“

”

MY FAVORITE MATERIAL IS LIGHT

& OTHER QUOTES BY ARCHITECTS

Φ

PREFACE

Vhile architects are best known or the buildings they design, many are lso writers, professors, and eloquent peakers—their opinions, advice, and erspectives as much a part of their egacy as their structural creations. This ompendium draws together the words f over two hundred architects across time nd around the world—from New York o Lagos, Sydney to Karachi, Tokyo to Oslo. 'hey reveal their thoughts on subjects s wide-ranging as beauty, the creative rocess, light, materials, money, scale, nd more. What emerges is a deeply uman portrait of what it means, and ow it feels, to experience the unique atisfactions and challenges of being an rchitect—of creating work that impacts he way we all move through the world.

Gender and racial inequities have ng persisted in the field of architecture, as as the entrenched image of the lone genius s the solitary force behind the world's ıost iconic buildings. This collection athers an increasingly diverse range of oices who have shaped—and continue to hape—our built environment, their words iscovered in monographs, interviews, ıemoirs, essays, letter collections, and ther sources. For those inspired to read ıe quotations in context, source notes can e found in the back of the book.

We hear about their childhood ıemories—how early they started nagining spaces, constructing bridges cross bathtubs, and looking up at their favorite buildings. Before he could hold a pencil, Oscar Niemeyer was drawing in the air with his fingers. Francis Kéré experienced his first sense of architecture huddled close to his grandmother, listening to her stories and feeling the safety of that enclosed space. When Camilla Block was about nine, she saw the Sydney Opera House for the first time. She remembers thinking, "What the hell is that?"

We learn how these individuals approach new projects, where they find their inspiration, and their feelings about collaboration. Frank Lloyd Wright believed that "the committee meeting" always led to compromise, while in Amanda Levete's London office, colleagues and clients alike are asked to remove their shoes—"the mess of the shoes" symbolizing that "we're all in it together."

We also discover vulnerabilities and personal insights. Gio Ponti was disturbed by pyramids, and Eduardo Souto de Moura was afraid of windows when he first started out. If she hadn't dedicated herself to architecture, Zaha Hadid imagined herself as a singer, politician, or psychologist.

"My favorite material is light" is a quote by American architect Steven Holl. In five words, Holl reframes light as a tangible material, an element that can be shaped and sculpted. That is, in a sense, the hope for this collection: that through this collage of quotations, we see architecture, and those who create our built world, with fresh eyes.

THERE IS NO AMOUNT OF MONEY, OR PRESTIGE, THAT WILL MAKE YOU FEEL GOOD ABOUT NOT STAYING TRUE TO YOUR ETHOS.

TATIANA BILBAO

I THINK "JOY" IS THE KEY WORD IN OUR WORK.

LOUIS KAHN

ALWAYS HAVE A VISION. HAVE AN IDEA ABOUT HOW YOUR WORK CAN CONTRIBUTE TO THE WORLD. WITHOUT A VISION, OTHERS WILL CONSUME YOUR WORK WITHOUT FURTHER CONTRIBUTING TO THE WORLD THEMSELVES.

HITOSHI ABE

YOUR BODY IS YOUR DESIGN TOOL. CULTIVATE YOUR ABILITY TO "READ" A PLACE BY CULTIVATING YOUR ABILITY TO PERCEIVE ALL THE INFORMATION YOU RECEIVE THROUGH ALL YOUR SENSES.

CARME PIGEM

YOU HAVE TO BE A GOOD LISTENER.

RENZO PIANO

LADIES AND GENTLEMEN, IF I SHOULD SAY WHAT IS THE MOST IMPORTANT TASK OF OUR TIME, I WOULD SAY IT IS TO SELECT.

MARCEL BREUER

Go in person to the lumber yard; choose your specimen and you will have your own wood that nobody else has.

GIO PONTI

Never demolish. Never subtract, remove, or replace. Always add, transform, and utilize, with and for the inhabitants.

ANNE LACATON AND JEAN-PHILIPPE VASSAL

YOU SHOULD NOT BUILD UNLESS YOU CAN GIVE BACK 100 PERCENT OF THE GREENERY YOU'RE DISRUPTING.

EMILIO AMBASZ

THERE'S ONLY ONE THING IN LIFE THAT YOU CANNOT DESIGN, AND THAT IS HERITAGE. IT IS REALLY IMPORTANT TO REMEMBER THAT.

AMANDA LEVETE

GET A CONTRACT SIGNED PRIOR TO STARTING WORK.

AMALE ANDRAOS

THE VALUE OF A GOOD ACCOUNTANT AND LAWYER WILL BE WITH YOU FOR MANY YEARS TO COME.

TOSIN OSHINOWO

The advice that I always give to young architects is to read EVERYTHING.

MICHAEL GRAVES

WITHOUT OBSESSION AND STUBBORNNESS, YOU CAN'T INNOVATE.

PATRICIA URQUIOLA

Work with people outside your discipline, see how they think, and let those conversations shape your approach. It's about building relationships, not just adopting aesthetics.

ALEX MUSTONEN

KEEP AT IT. IN ARCHITECTURE YOU NEVER BURN OUT YOUNG.

DAN WOOD

NEVER LET OTHERS SET THE LIMITS FOR YOU.

FARSHID MOUSSAVI

OPTIMISM IS AN IMPORTANT ACCOMPLICE.

GABRIELA CARRILLO

BE PATIENT AND DON'T TRY TO FIND THE SHORTCUT.

ROSSANA HU

There's no task that you're ever asked to do that doesn't have a richness of insight you can gain if you put your heart and soul into it. There's nothing too insignificant to not become something that tells you about design in a better way.

MARION WEISS

YOU DO BETTER WORK WHEN YOU ARE KIND TO YOURSELF.

FLORA SAMUEL

SELECT A PARTNER WHO WILL SUPPORT YOUR CAREER AND SHARE THE RESPONSIBILITY OF RAISING A FAMILY.

ALEXANDRA HAGEN

HAVING THE STAMINA TO KEEP AT IT MATTERS. STICKING WITH SOMETHING NOT JUST FOR THE MONTH BUT FOR YEARS. BENDING, NOT BREAKING. AND ALWAYS PAYING IT FORWARD.

LESLEY LOKKO

TRUST THE INVISIBLE.

DANIEL LIBESKIND

THE ONLY REAL ADVICE I WOULD HAVE FOR MY YOUNGER SELF WOULD BE TO SLEEP A LOT MORE AND PRODUCE JUST A LITTLE LESS.

MÓNICA PONCE DE LEÓN

DON'T EVER TURN DOWN A JOB BECAUSE IT'S BENEATH YOU, [OR] BECAUSE YOU THINK YOU WANT TO DO SOMETHING LARGER.

JULIA MORGAN

IF YOU HAVE ANY IDEALISM, YOU MUST EXPRESS IT.

STEVEN HOLL

DON'T YOU EVER BELIEVE AN OLD MAN WHEN HE SAYS THAT SOMETHING CANNOT BE DONE.

WALTER GROPIUS

THERE IS AN INFINITE NUMBER OF UNTOLD STORIES AND UNDREAMT WORLDS WAITING TO HAPPEN FROM YOUR UNIQUE VOICE AND YOUR UNIQUE PERSPECTIVE.

SUMAYYA VALLY

SELF-BELIEF IS IMPORTANT. YOU MAY THINK THAT YOU CAN'T DO IT, BUT ACTUALLY YOU CAN.

ALISON BROOKS

BELIEVE IN GOOD FORTUNE, AND MAKE THE MOST OF IT WHEN IT OCCURS.

JOHN WARDLE

BEGIN TODAY!

CHARLES RENNIE MACKINTOSH

AN ARCHITECT'S DUTY IS TO CONVERT FEELINGS INTO PHYSICAL FORM.

TADAO ANDO

Architects have been doing virtual reality for over two thousand years. I always think of it as designing a thing that has yet to be specified or realized.

GREG LYNN

WE HAVE THE OPPORTUNITY AND RESPONSIBILITY TO MAKE THE WORLD A LITTLE MORE LIKE OUR DREAMS.

BJARKE INGELS

YOU'VE GOT TO HAVE GUTS TO BE AN ARCHITECT!

FRANK LLOYD WRIGHT

I don't believe in the image of the architect or the studio. I think we as architects are ordinary people, but what we do is not ordinary. Our work is important, not us—we are here today, gone tomorrow, but the work stays whether we like it or not.

KASHEF CHOWDHURY

That period of the heroic single male figure is over. It's more a time of collaboration, and a deeper contemplation about what buildings can mean and how they can have more social value.

ELIZABETH DILLER

I THINK THE ROLE OF THE ARCHITECT IN GENERAL SHOULD BE CHANGED.

YASMEEN LARI

THE ARCHITECT'S RESPONSIBILITY EXTENDS BEYOND THE CLIENT'S BRIEF INTO THE PUBLIC REALM SO THAT HIS BUILDINGS, WHETHER SMALL OR LARGE, GIVE PUBLIC PERFORMANCES TO THE USER AND PASSERBY—THE AUDIENCE OF TODAY AND TOMORROW.

RICHARD ROGERS

BEING AN ARCHITECT IS LIKE YOU'RE AN ACTOR, AND YOU CONTROL HOW YOU WANT PEOPLE TO FEEL. FOR ME, CREATING FORM IS LIKE AN ACTING TECHNIQUE.

MA YANSONG

The most radical architectural imaginators indulge personal fantasy while interpreting reality and aspiring to universality.

LISA LANDRUM

WHAT WE MAKE MAKES US.

ANUPAMA KUNDOO

ARCHITECTURE CANNOT SAVE THE WORLD, BUT IT CAN ACT AS A GOOD EXAMPLE.

ALVAR AALTO

THE MEASURE OF SUCCESS IN ARCHITECTURE IS AN ARCHITECTURE THAT MAKES YOU FEEL BETTER ABOUT YOURSELF, ABOUT THE PLACE YOU'RE IN, THAT LIFTS YOU.

AMANDA LEVETE

ARCHITECTURE ITSELF HAS A VERY IMPORTANT ROLE TO PLAY IN MAKING PEOPLE FEEL VALUED.

ALISON BROOKS

I DESIGN BY PUTTING HUMANS IN THE CENTER AND CARING ABOUT THEM. SPACES NEED TO NOT ONLY HAVE THE CAPACITY TO PROTECT OUR BODIES, BUT TO INSPIRE OUR LIVES.

TATIANA BILBAO

Buildings—contrary to popular thought—are not inanimate objects. They live and breathe, and like humans have an outside and an inside, a body and a soul. So how does one go about designing a building that can sing? A building that expresses character, humanity, and beauty?

DANIEL LIBESKIND

An urge for comfort must be the basis for all architecture if a harmony shall be achieved between the spaces that are made and the activities that will take place in them.

JØRN UTZON

I BELIEVE IN AN "EMOTIONAL ARCHITECTURE." IT IS VERY IMPORTANT FOR HUMANKIND THAT ARCHITECTURE SHOULD MOVE BY ITS BEAUTY.

LUIS BARRAGÁN

The term "actionable idealism" came about because I was trying to describe the intention behind our practice. Architecture can be a catalyst to help transform things, to make positive change. I believe that. I've seen it.

JEANNE GANG

I AM TOTALLY UNINTERESTED IN THE IDEA THAT ARCHITECTURE REPRESENTS THE ARCHITECT. I AM INTERESTED IN "RESPONSIVE ARCHITECTURE."

FARSHID MOUSSAVI

ARCHITECTURE CAN BE MANY THINGS, BUT IT SHOULD BE APPROPRIATE. IT SHOULD HAVE CULTURAL RELEVANCE.

ROBERT VENTURI

IT'S NOT ONLY THE FUNCTION THAT MUST BE MET BUT ALSO AN ARTISTIC AMBITION; GOOD ARCHITECTURE IS A TOTAL WORK OF ART.

DAVID MARQUARDT

IT IS NECESSARY THAT THE WORK DOES NOT FALL FROM THE SKY OVER ITS INHABITANTS, BUT RATHER EXPRESSES A NEED.

LINA BO BARDI

ARCHITECTURE IS THE MASTERLY, CORRECT, AND MAGNIFICENT PLAY OF MASSES BROUGHT TOGETHER IN LIGHT.

LE CORBUSIER

Architecture is a fuzzy amalgamation of ancient knowledge and contemporary practice, an awkward way to look at the world and an inadequate medium to operate on it.

REM KOOLHAAS

MY CONCEPT
OF ARCHITECTURE
IS THAT IT IS INVISIBLE.
IT'S INTANGIBLE.
BUT I BELIEVE IT CAN
BE FELT THROUGH
THE FIVE SENSES.

ARATA ISOZAKI

ARCHITECTURE IS
ABOUT MANIPULATING
MATTER UNTIL
THE SPIRIT EMERGES
FROM IT.

LIU JIAKUN

I THINK GREAT ARCHITECTURE SHOULD BE EVERYONE'S RIGHT, LIKE FRESH WATER AND HEALTH.

SARAH WIGGLESWORTH

Architecture is how people meet in space.

KAZUYO SEJIMA

Architecture creates spatial legacies for living in. Whether these legacies are good or bad depends on whether the architect prioritizes people or product during the process of creating them.

HARRIET HARRISS

Architecture has nothing to do with taste, and paradoxically, not even with proportions, it is more brutal on the one hand, and more complex on the other. In any case, the analysis of the problem is the basis of everything.

PATRICIA VIEL

ARCHITECTURE IS THE PLAY BETWEEN KNOWLEDGE AND INTUITION, LOGIC AND THE SPIRIT, THE MEASURABLE AND THE UNMEASURABLE.

RICHARD ROGERS

THE POWER OF ARCHITECTURE IS THE POWER OF SYNTHESIS, TO SAY WHAT YOU WANT IN TWO WORDS INSTEAD OF THREE, TO ACHIEVE A SOLUTION IN AS FEW MOVES AS POSSIBLE.

ALEJANDRO ARAVENA

ARCHITECTURE IS A PROCESS OF TRANSLATION.

YVONNE FARRELL

NO MATTER WHERE YOU ARE, ARCHITECTURE IS A PROCESS OF DISCOVERY. IT'S NOT JUST SPACE-MAKING; IT'S ABOUT DISCUSSION AND HOW YOU TURN DESIRE INTO FORM.

MARIAM ISSOUFOU

Architecture can get us closer to one another, to the living, to nature and to our environment, essentially allowing us to live synchronized with the beauty of this world.

LINA GHOTMEH

TO ME, ARCHITECTURE IS ALWAYS A BACKGROUND FOR CELEBRATING LIFE.

ANUPAMA KUNDOO

ALL BUILDING IS NOT ARCHITECTURE.

LOUIS KAHN

I LOVE ARCHITECTURE BUT HATE A LOT OF BUILDINGS.

ELADIA SMOKE

There is a defining, magical moment when the building is born and claims a life of its own.

SUMAYA DABBAGH

ARCHITECTURE MUST MOVE YOU, PERIOD!

MARCIO KOGAN

I THINK THE CHANCE OF FINDING BEAUTY IS HIGHER IF YOU DON'T WORK ON IT DIRECTLY.

PETER ZUMTHOR

ALL OF US NEED BEAUTY TO EVOLVE.

TATIANA BILBAO

WE BELIEVE IN DESIGNING FOR LIFE, WHICH IN TURN, LEADS US TO DESIGN FOR BEAUTY.

MARIO CUCINELLA

I THINK THAT WE SHOULD HAVE MORE BEAUTY AND BALANCE AND NURTURING IN OUR ENVIRONMENTS.

DOUGLAS CARDINAL

I spent my childhood (during World War II) at my grandfather's farm, and I never heard anyone in that community use the word "beautiful." But everything that they made was beautiful and turned into beauty.

JUHANI PALLASMAA

BEAUTY IS AN ORACLE THAT SPEAKS TO ALL.

LUIS BARRAGÁN

I AM NOT INTERESTED IN BEAUTY.

PETER EISENMAN

SOME ARCHITECTURE IS EASY TO LIKE. OURS FRIGHTENS SOME PEOPLE.

DENISE SCOTT BROWN

I LOVE THINGS THAT ARE OFF, A BIT TOO FAT OR TOO THIN OR TOO LONG OR TOO SHORT.

ELIZABETH DILLER

I LOVE THINGS WHICH ARE BROKEN AND THEN REASSEMBLED, AS IN ARCHAEOLOGICAL AND SURGICAL OPERATIONS.

ALDO ROSSI

BEAUTY IS THE PEAK OF FUNCTIONALITY!

ÁLVARO SIZA

REAL BEAUTY IS NOT A CONCEPTION OF FORM WHICH CAN BE TAUGHT, IT IS THE RESULT OF HARMONY BETWEEN SEVERAL INTRINSIC FACTORS, NOT LEAST THE SOCIAL.

ALVAR AALTO

THE PUBLIC OFTEN THINKS THAT A BUILDING CAN BE FUNCTIONAL, BUT UGLY AS HELL. TO ME, THAT'S IMPOSSIBLE. IF IT FUNCTIONS PROPERLY—NOT JUST IN TERMS OF "THE PLUMBING WORKS," BUT IN THE WAY IT SERVES THE ACTIVITIES OF THE BUILDING—IT IS BEAUTIFUL.

MOSHE SAFDIE

It's important to me that when people spend time in my buildings, they don't just experience comfort and functionality. They have to be infused with beauty and they should be surprised.

MANUELLE GAUTRAND

TAKE NOTHING FOR GRANTED AS BEAUTIFUL OR UGLY, BUT TAKE EVERY BUILDING TO PIECES, AND CHALLENGE EVERY FEATURE.

FRANK LLOYD WRIGHT

Beauty will result from the form and correspondence of the whole, with respect to the several parts, of the parts with regard to each other, and of these again to the whole; that the structure may appear an entire and complete body, wherein each member agrees with the other, and all necessary to compose what you intend to form.

ANDREA PALLADIO

FOR ME, BEAUTY IS SYNONYMOUS WITH SUSTAINABILITY.

ANNA HERINGER

I'VE ALWAYS WANTED TO BE AN ARCHITECT.

TOSIN OSHINOWO

WHEN I WAS FIVE, IT WAS A DIFFERENT TIME AND I COULD WALK TO KINDERGARTEN AND WALK THE CITY STREETS. I WOULD GO OUT OF MY WAY TO LOOK AT PARTICULAR BUILDINGS.

PATRICK STEWART

I WAS VERY MUCH INTERESTED IN IMAGINING SPACES FROM A YOUNG AGE, AND MY FIRST PROJECT WAS A HOUSE FOR A PUPPET MADE FROM PAPER BOXES.

PATRICIA VIEL

Our parlor ceiling was uncomfortably high, and so I used to sit and play under the grand piano. The low headroom under our piano provided me the coziest place I knew.

RICHARD NEUTRA

SOMETIMES I CAN ALMOST FEEL A PARTICULAR DOOR HANDLE IN MY HAND, A PIECE OF METAL SHAPED LIKE THE BACK OF A SPOON. I USED TO TAKE HOLD OF IT WHEN I WENT INTO MY AUNT'S GARDEN.

PETER ZUMTHOR

WHEN I WAS ABOUT NINE, I CAME TO SYDNEY. WE CAME TO SEE THE OPERA HOUSE. I REMEMBER THAT PROFOUND FEELING OF THINKING, WOW . . . WHAT THE HELL IS THAT?

CAMILLA BLOCK

One of my earliest memories is of lying on my back on a cushion on the floor underneath the baby grand piano we had at home. While my mother played the piano above me, I remember being aware of the wonderful space filled with music under that walnut instrument.

YVONNE FARRELL

MY GRANDMOTHER BROUGHT THE WOOD BLOCKS HOME FOR THE FIRE, FOR THE WOOD STOVE. AND SHE WOULD THROW THEM ON THE FLOOR AND MAKE CITIES WITH ME.

FRANK GEHRY

WHEN I WAS VERY LITTLE MY MOTHER SAID I USED TO DRAW IN THE AIR WITH MY FINGERS.

OSCAR NIEMEYER

MY MOTHER'S FRIENDS WOULD COME OVER, AND I WOULD DRAW MICKEY MOUSE AND DONALD DUCK FOR THEM. THEY WOULD ASK WHAT I WANTED TO BE WHEN I GREW UP, AND I WOULD SAY, "AN ARTIST."

MICHAEL GRAVES

Some vivid memories were with time spent with my grandmother—we would sit and draw what we call sections, with a blue ballpoint pen on small scraps of paper.

HILARY SAMPLE

I was obsessed with making bridges—between tables, along the arms of sofas, making spans between furniture and across the bath.

NICHOLAS GRIMSHAW

When I was a child, we used to go up to Ta'if in the mountains on the weekends. Moving between the flatness and openness of Jeddah to the forms created by the jagged hills of Ta'if would excite and inspire me.

SUMAYA DABBAGH

WHEN I WAS TWELVE, I COULD ALREADY CONSTRUCT PERSPECTIVE DRAWINGS AND DRAW AXONOMETRIC PROJECTIONS.

GREG LYNN

WHEN I WAS ELEVEN OR TWELVE, I ENCOUNTERED A BOOK ABOUT LE CORBUSIER. THAT WAS WHEN I REALIZED ARCHITECTURE WAS A CREATIVE ACTIVITY. BEFORE THAT, ARCHITECTURE WAS JUST BUILDINGS.

SOU FUJIMOTO

I left school at thirteen-and-a-half to serve a three years' apprenticeship to an engraver. At seventeen I was lucky enough to meet a man unburdened with prejudices, who ultimately entrusted me with the construction of his house.

LE CORBUSIER

While I was growing up my parents moved homes often. . . . No one in the family was excited about moving except for me—it meant rearranging the house and the furniture and this was exciting and full of new possibilities.

RAHUL MEHROTRA

I REMEMBER THE ROOM WHERE MY GRANDMOTHER WOULD SIT AND TELL STORIES WITH A LITTLE LIGHT, WHILE WE WOULD HUDDLE CLOSE TO EACH OTHER, AND HER VOICE INSIDE THE ROOM ENCLOSED US, SUMMONING US TO COME CLOSER AND FORM A SAFE PLACE. THIS WAS MY FIRST SENSE OF ARCHITECTURE.

FRANCIS KÉRÉ

Back then, it wasn't unusua to walk home from school in temperatures of up to 45 degrees [113 degrees Fahrenheit]. I'll never forge the feeling of stepping insid our cool mud house.

MARIAM ISSOUFOU

When I was a kid, I was ver interested in other people's houses and how they lived In a way, architecture became a window into othe people's lives, more than space and buildings.

KONSTANTINOS PANTAZIS

I was fourteen, and had an older friend who got into Cooper Union to study architecture. We'd walk around my neighborhood i Douglaston, Queens, and loc at the elevation of houses. We'd try to figure out their layouts and draw them.

DEBORAH BERKE

WHEN OTHER BOYS WERE PLAYING FOOTBALL, I WAS IN MY ROOM, DRAWING WHOLE WORLDS—PEOPLE, BUILDINGS, CIVILIZATIONS THAT DID NOT EXIST.

OLIVIER MARTY

BY SECOND OR THIRD GRADE, I WAS DOING MY OWN THING. I STILL RESENT BEING TOLD WHAT TO DO IN ANY WAY, SHAPE, OR FORM.

MAYA LIN

One day, as a small boy, I was copying the portrait of Napoleon. His left eye was giving me trouble. Already I had erased the drawing of it several times. My father leaned over and lovingly corrected my work. I threw the paper and pencil across the room, saying, "Now it is your drawing, not mine." Two cannot make a single drawing.

LOUIS KAHN

I LOOK AT PICTURES OF MYSELF WHEN I WAS A KID, AND I LOOK TOTALLY THE SAME. I WAS VERY CLEAR ON HOW I WOULD DRESS AND TOTALLY CLEAR ON WHAT MY ROOM LOOKED LIKE. I WAS SUPER SPECIFIC.

ANNABELLE SELLDORF

YOU KNOW, WE THINK THAT PEOPLE BECOME INDIVIDUALS ONLY LATER IN LIFE, AND THAT CHILDREN ARE UNMOLDED, BUT YOU CAN SEE, CAN'T YOU, THAT THEY ARE INDIVIDUALS VERY EARLY ON.

ZAHA HADID

THERE IS NO GOOD BUILDING WITH A BAD CLIENT.

EDUARDO SOUTO DE MOURA

I WOULD NEVER DESIGN A HOUSE THAT I WANT TO DESIGN. . . . I ALWAYS TRY TO DESIGN A HOUSE THEY WANT BUT THROUGH MY EYES. THIS IS A VERY SUBTLE DIFFERENCE THAT IS VERY IMPORTANT TO ME.

ISAY WEINFELD

OF COURSE WE DO NOT PARTICIPATE IN ANY PROJECT WHERE WE FUNDAMENTALLY REJECT THE VALUES OF THE CLIENT.

REM KOOLHAAS

I need to truly understand what my clients want and who they are before we create. I take a deep dive into their lives; I connect with them in a very human way.

VINCENT VAN DUYSEN

Rather than "educating" clients, I find it most effective to experienc things together—such as visiting buildings we have designed—so they ca feel it firsthand.

KEIJI ASHIZAWA

PEOPLE HAVE ALWAYS BEEN THE MOST IMPORTANT.... AND THAT'S BECAUSE YOU CARE FOR WHOM YOU'RE DESIGNING FOR.

FRANCINE HOUBEN

RESIDENTS NEED TO BE REAL PARTNERS, AND NOT JUST ASKED WHICH COLORS TO CHOOSE.

ANNE LACATON

NEVER TALK TO A CLIENT ABOUT ARCHITECTURE. TALK TO HIM ABOUT HIS CHILDREN. THAT IS SIMPLY GOOD POLITICS. HE WILL NOT UNDERSTAND WHAT YOU HAVE TO SAY ABOUT ARCHITECTURE MOST OF THE TIME.

MIES VAN DER ROHE

ONE OF THE SECRETS YOU LEARN AS AN ARCHITECT IS THAT WHEN THE CLIENTS COME TO YOU WITH REQUIREMENTS, YOU SHOULD DOUBLE THE AMOUNT OF MONEY THEY CLAIM THEY HAVE AND HALVE THE AMOUNT OF SPACE THEY BELIEVE THEY NEED.

EMILIO AMBASZ

THIS IS REALLY WHERE THE BIG CHALLENGE LIES: TO TRY TO ABSORB WHAT THE CLIENT IS DREAMING OF WITHOUT COMPROMISING WHAT YOU CONSIDER TO BE A GOOD IDEA. . . .

KARIM NADER

Quite a lot of people think that being an architect is the same as being an artist, but we always need the approval of a client because the client is spending the money.

ELLEN VAN LOON

CLIENTS! WE REALLY BADLY NEED A SCHOOL FOR CLIENTS.

DENISE SCOTT BROWN

I have always been in the fortunate position of working for respectable clients who, in complete contrast to the State, understand that an artist has to live by his work and that it is hardly dignified to turn him into a beggar.

ANTONI GAUDÍ

YOU CANNOT MAKE A GOOD BUILDING WITHOUT ONE PERSON WHO HAS PERSPECTIVE AND WHO SEES IN YOUR PROJECT A REPRESENTATION AND EXPRESSION OF THAT VISION AND WHO PROTECTS IT AND SUPPORTS IT SO THAT IT BECOMES A REALITY.

SHELLEY MCNAMARA

I STARTED WORKING FOR ANDY WARHOL WHO WAS AT HIS HEIGHT IN THE 70S. THE SECOND CLIENT WAS YVES SAINT LAURENT, AGNELLI THE THIRD, AND FOURTH, ROTHSCHILD. IT WAS LUCKY.

PETER MARINO

I TRY TO MAINTAIN A BALANCE BETWEEN WORKING FOR CLIENTS WHO ARE WELL OFF AND THOSE WHO AREN'T.

SHIGERU BAN

I OFTEN TELL MY COLLEAGUES, "LET US NOT TREAT DISASTER-AFFECTED HOUSEHOLDS AS DESTITUTE, NEEDING HANDOUTS. RATHER LET US GIVE THEM DUE RESPECT AND TREAT THEM AS WE WOULD A CORPORATE-SECTOR CLIENT."

YASMEEN LARI

I DON'T THINK YOU'RE SUCCESSFUL IF YOU CAN'T CALL YOUR CLIENT BACK UP AND SAY, "I'M COMING OUT TO SEE THE HOUSE."

SAMUEL MOCKBEE

ARCHITECTURE IS TOO IMPORTANT TO BE LEFT TO ARCHITECTS ALONE.

NORMAN FOSTER

THERE IS NO IMMACULATE CONCEPTION OF IDEAS. COLLABORATION IS THE TRUTH OF ARCHITECTURE.

DENISE SCOTT BROWN

I THINK THE COLLECTIVE INTELLIGENCE IS GREATER THAN THE INDIVIDUAL'S INTELLIGENCE.

KUNLÉ ADEYEMI

I still have a pencil in my pocket and I love the sense of surprise of teamwork and having young people around me. My office is not just my own, it's also the office of 160 people.

RENZO PIANO

Our design process alway includes collaborative brainstorming amongst a group of the 140 designers in my firm, wh are also artists, sculptors, chefs, opera singers, architects, playwrights, and set designers.

DAVID ROCKWELL

IT'S A VERY FLAT HIERARCHY. EVERYONE DOES EVERYTHING. THERE'S NO ONE IN THE OFFICE WHO JUST DOES ONE THING.

JAMES DALLMAN

THINKING COLLECTIVELY ABOUT VERY COMPLEX ISSUES IS AN EXTRAORDINARY DRIVING PROCESS. SOMETIMES, IT CAN BE THE LEAST IMPORTANT SENTENCE IN A MEETING ROOM THAT ACTUALLY CREATES A NECESSARY SOLUTION.

KJETIL TRÆDAL THORSEN

I DON'T HAVE AN OFFICE WHERE I DISAPPEAR. I'M PARKED ALONGSIDE MY COLLEAGUES, SO THERE'S NO APPARENT DIFFERENCE BETWEEN AN INTERN OUT OF HIGH SCHOOL AND MYSELF. WHEN YOU ERASE THOSE DISTANCES, YOU GET TO HAVE FUN.

DANIEL LIBESKIND

THE “COMMITTEE MEETING” NEVER PRODUCED ANYTHING IN ARCHITECTURE ABOVE THE LEVEL OF A COMPROMISE.

FRANK LLOYD WRIGHT

I would prefer not to work with other people. I work with larger firms of architects in different ways but I don’t discuss my ideas with them. I would never do that.

MIES VAN DER ROHE

How do three people do creative work? Our answer was that it is like the interplay of a jazz trio.

CARME PIGEM

WE HAVE TO STOP THINKING THAT ARCHITECTURE IS SOMETHING THAT YOU CAN REALLY MANAGE AND DO BY YOURSELF.

PATRICIA VIEL

WE HAVE A RULE THAT EVERYONE TAKES OFF THEIR SHOES, EVEN OUR CLIENTS. FOR ME THE MESS OF THE SHOES IS EMBLEMATIC OF THE SENSE THAT WE'RE ALL IN IT TOGETHER.

AMANDA LEVETE

Understand the importance of trusting others. Learn from the skills and experience of other people. Teamwork is very important.

ZAHA HADID

Competition is not the only way to go about receiving a commission— the Aboriginal people survived by cooperation, not through competition, as opposed to the Darwinian survival of the fittest.

GLENN MURCUTT

IN THE PAST SO MANY BEAUTIFUL BUILDINGS WERE LITERALLY PRODUCED THROUGH BLOOD, SWEAT, AND STARK INEQUALITY. WE AIM TO MAKE BEAUTIFUL BUILDINGS IN A COLLABORATIVE, FAIR WAY WITH POSITIVE OUTCOMES FOR AS MANY PEOPLE AS POSSIBLE.

JUDE BARBER

ARCHITECTURE IS THE ART OF COLLABORATION.

LINA GHOTMEH

DIALOGUE IS THE ANSWER.

ÁLVARO SIZA

There is no house in the world that exists in isolation. Housing always exists in a village. Everyone is a member of a family.

RIKEN YAMAMOTO

IT TAKES A VILLAGE TO BUILD A VILLAGE.

TOSIN OSHINOWO

You have to bring a community with you when you're dealing with place-making. If you take sustainability to mean "something self-sustaining," we need people loving and caring for their environment and feeling that it's an expression of them, and that therefore it can be cared for and looked after.

SARAH WIGGLESWORTH

WHEN WE CAN, WE ALLOCATE GENEROUS TIME AT THE OUTSET OF A PROJECT TO GIVE OURSELVES THE PRIVILEGE OF HEARING LOCAL STORIES AND UNDERSTANDING LOCAL TRADITIONS. OUR DESIGNS ARE THEN VERY MUCH DERIVED FROM THOSE SHARED STORIES.

BRIAN PORTER

I ALWAYS TAKE MY CUE FROM THE COMMUNITY.

PATRICK STEWART

I am most proud of the women and men who believed in me for hours, days, weeks, who kept quarrying stone and working hard to provide the construction site with materials. They did this for someone very young, coming from the community but who went abroad and apparently learned something. They said, "We don't understand what it is, but we want to support him."

FRANCIS KÉRÉ

WHAT I REALLY LIKE IS SPEED. I AM ALSO FASCINATED BY FIGHTER JETS. AND, AS YOU MAY KNOW, I DESIGNED A BOAT.

ODILE DECQ

PYRAMIDS, BOTH LARGE AND SMALL, DISTURB ME.

GIO PONTI

I do not like ducts; I do not like pipes.

LOUIS KAHN

WHEN I STARTED WORKING AS AN ARCHITECT, I WAS AFRAID OF WINDOWS. WHEN I HAD TO DESIGN A WINDOW, I PANICKED.

EDUARDO SOUTO DE MOURA

I do read
Don Quixote
when I get totally
frustrated by
everyone screwing
with everything
and nothing seems
to make sense.

FRANK GEHRY

The female
philosopher
Hannah
Arendt is like
a spiritual
master to me.

RIKEN YAMAMOTO

People say architects are not supposed to like sports, but I'm an avid sports fan. Doing a stadium for me is like doing a cathedral.

PETER EISENMAN

SOME YEARS AGO, I WROTE A PIECE ABOUT ONE OF MY OBSESSIONS: THE MEDITATIONS OF MARCUS AURELIUS. I OWN 66 EDITIONS IN DIFFERENT LANGUAGES.

ALBERTO CAMPO BAEZA

I'M NOT OBSESSIVE ABOUT WRITING IMPLEMENTS LIKE SOME ARCHITECTS.

DEBORAH BERKE

When I was a child,
I really wanted
to be a grandmother.

KAZUYO SEJIMA

Many years ago,
I wanted to
become a singer.
I also think
I could have gone
into politics or
become a shrink.

ZAHA HADID

To this day I love to hold a handful of many-colored pencils and open my hand to see them lying loose upon my palm, in the light.

FRANK LLOYD WRIGHT

I love when people
give buildings
nicknames.

WOLF PRIX

SECRETLY, I'VE ALWAYS FELT IT NECESSARY TO DESIGN BUILDINGS WHERE MY DAD WOULD FEEL COMFORTABLE.

JULIE EIZENBERG

MY FAVORITE
OBJECT IS A
KALEIDOSCOPE.

MANUELLE GAUTRAND

I often dream of buildings, very often versions of places I've lived. These are recurring dreams, but where I discover rooms and spaces that were never there.

CHARLOTTE SKENE CATLING

I WANT TO DIE ON A CONSTRUCTION SITE.

RENZO PIANO

I WOULD
RATHER BE THE
PAINTER OF
THE SMALL
PAINTING ON
THE BOTTOM
OF THE ALTAR
THAN BE
THE GRAND
MAESTRO OF
THE CENTER
MASTERPIECE.

CARLO SCARPA

CREATIVE PROCESS

WHEN I START A PROJECT I TRY TO FAN OUT IN ALL DIRECTIONS.

JEANNE GANG

THE START OF THE PROCESS HAPPENS THROUGH DISCUSSION— LIKE AN INTERNAL PITCH MEETING.

ALEX MUSTONEN

When I'm working on a building, I often find myself poring over photographs of faces. When I designed the Jewish Museum in Berlin, for example, I sat for hours looking at images of people walking around Alexanderplatz in the 1930s.

DANIEL LIBESKIND

I ALWAYS RESEARCH SOMETHING FOR THREE MONTHS, A YEAR, SIX MONTHS. I THINK I DO IT BECAUSE IT'S AN INCUBATION PERIOD. AND IT'S ALSO BECAUSE I COME FROM A FAMILY OF ACADEMICS, AND I GUESS I MISS SCHOOL.

MAYA LIN

I take lots of notes during Zooms, but never file them and don't know what they relate to in the end. The act of writing somehow gets the information to stick, but the papers are just kind of junk.

ELIZABETH DILLER

First I gather and synthesize all the possible elements related to the people who I am going to work with and the history of the place. That's my structuralist background. Then I get into bed, put on my mask, and put in my earplugs and wait in the silence and the dark for it to come.

JEAN NOUVEL

When the projects are of a highly complex nature, they need to be "assimilated slowly"; knowledge has to be stored up, and you must know how to wait in silence, perhaps wandering around the chosen site with your hands in your pockets.

RENZO PIANO

Nearly every design task involves tens, often hundreds, sometimes thousands of different contradictory elements, which are forced into a functional harmony only by man's will. This harmony cannot be achieved by any other means than those of art.

ALVAR AALTO

I'M REMINDED OF HOW STONES ARE MADE ROUND AND SMOOTH BY THE MOTION OF THE SEA AND BY THE PASSAGE OF TIME. IN THE SAME WAY, WE TRY TO WORK WITH OUR IDEAS TO FIND THE ROUNDED AND SMOOTH "STONE" OF A REFINED IDEA.

YVONNE FARRELL

WHAT'S EXCITING FOR US IS TO NEVER FEEL SETTLED. WE'RE ALWAYS TESTING.

CAMILLA BLOCK

IN EACH PROJECT WE BEGIN WITH INFORMATION AND DISORDER, CONFUSION OF PURPOSE, PROGRAM AMBIGUITY, INFINITY OF MATERIALS AND FORMS. ALL OF THESE ELEMENTS, LIKE OBFUSCATING SMOKE, SWIRL IN A NERVOUS ATMOSPHERE. ARCHITECTURE IS A RESULT OF ACTING ON THIS INDETERMINACY.

STEVEN HOLL

HERE IN THE OFFICE, WE SAY, "WHAT IF?" A LOT. THAT'S HOW WE OFTEN TITLE OUR PROJECTS IN THE VERY BEGINNING, "WHAT IF?"

RICK JOY

I GO SWIMMING TWICE A WEEK AND I WALK UP FIVE FLOORS TO MY APARTMENT (THERE IS NO ELEVATOR), AND LIKE GOYA, I'M STILL LEARNING.

ALBERTO CAMPO BAEZA

I listen to a lot of music, and a lot of jazz, because jazz has this combination that is very important for us architects. . . . It has a great spontaneity and freshness, but also a solid structure.

ÁLVARO SIZA

MY GRANDMOTHER INTRODUCED ME TO THE MUSIC OF ENRICO CARUSO AS A CHILD AND IT STUCK. I NOW HAVE A COLLECTION OF 12,000 RECORDS.

RICHARD ENGLAND

WEDNESDAY IS MY DAY. IF I AM KEEN ON PICKING UP A NEW LANGUAGE, WEDNESDAY IS THE DAY FOR THAT. DANCING OR SINGING? WEDNESDAY IS WHEN I DIVE INTO THOSE PURSUITS.

GLORIA CABRAL

I'M AN EXTREME SKIER, A DANCER, AND VERY INTERESTED IN PHYSICS AND THE METAPHYSICAL.

CAZÚ ZEGERS

Flight for me is a developing passion—just like architecture. My log books detail more than 4,500 hours in the air.

NORMAN FOSTER

I LOVE FLOATING IN THE WATER.

RENZO PIANO

I LOVE TO COOK.

TATIANA BILBAO

I WOULDN'T SAY IT IS A MOTTO, BUT EVERY MORNING I TELL MYSELF TO TRY AND COME HOME EARLY!

PATRICIA VIEL

I DRAW. IT GOES FASTER THAN WORDS.

JEAN NOUVEL

The Creator created paper for drawing architecture on. Everything else is, at least for my part, to misuse paper.

ALVAR AALTO

THE PLEASURE OF DRAWING AND DETAILING IS IN OUR DNA. INFINITE SHEETS OF PAPER ARE DRAFTED FOR EACH PROJECT.

MARCIO KOGAN

I THINK WE ALL START WITH INTUITIVE DOODLES WHICH EVENTUALLY EXPRESS OURSELVES. I KNOW THAT SOMEHOW I GET A DESIGN SUDDENLY.

LOUIS KAHN

EVERY MEETING WITH A CLIENT, BUILDER, CONSULTANT GROUP, OR OTHER ARCHITECTS IS A DUEL OF SORTS, SOMETIMES FRIENDLY. IF YOU CAN'T DRAW YOU ARE UNARMED.

CAMILLA BLOCK

Most of the drawings I make are done on the back of used paper. They all end up in the trash, except for a few I decide to use for publication.

SMILJAN RADIĆ

MY SKETCHES ARE NOT PRECIOUS.

ELIZABETH DILLER

DRAWINGS SERVE SCALE, PROPORTION, AND COMPOSITION. DRAWINGS DON'T LIE—RENDERINGS DO.

ANNABELLE SELLDORF

The verb "to draw" means "to bring out," and to bring out is to reveal, and to reveal is to understand. With the computer, you arrive at the end before you comprehend the meaning of that end.

GLENN MURCUTT

I don't use the computer. I do sketches, very quickly, often more than 100 on the same formal research.

ZAHA HADID

My staff has to be able to hand-draw their intentions to make it at my firm. We use and love the computer, and we love the immediacy of drawing on Trace. We work back and forth.

MARLON BLACKWELL

We begin designing with paper models and pencil drawings. Lots of them.

KAZUYO SEJIMA

It's a complex thing, a drawing: it transforms itself and is never as one imagined it to start with. Drawing is an adventure that fascinates and sustains me.

CLAUDE PARENT

FOR ME, DRAWING IS MEDICINE, MEANING THAT IT'S A WAY TO MAKE MYSELF FEEL BETTER.

CHRIS CORNELIUS

THE SKETCH IS VERY QUICK AND ALWAYS RETAINS ITS FUNCTION, LIKE A SUPPORT, IDEALLY UNTIL THE LAST STONE OF A BUILDING IS LAID.

ÁLVARO SIZA

THE DRAWN LINE IS ONE OF THE GREAT HUMAN INVENTIONS, AND IT IS AVAILABLE TO ALL OF US—A TOOL BOTH COMMON AND ESOTERIC, PERSONAL AND UNIVERSAL.

LEBBEUS WOODS

On an airplane, I do so much of my sketching just looking down at landscapes, both manmade—like looking down at the crop circles—as well as when you're going over the West, the Rocky Mountains.

MAYA LIN

EVERY LINE AN ARCHITECT DRAWS, THEY DRAW IT FOR EVERY CONSCIOUSNESS. THEY THINK, IS THIS A BEAUTIFUL LINE? IS IT A GOOD LINE? OR DOES IT JUST NEED TO MOVE THREE CENTIMETERS?

ELLEN VAN LOON

SOMETIMES, I CAN BE WORKING ON A DRAWING FOR WEEKS, MAKING HUNDREDS OF SKETCHES, WHEN, WITH NO WARNING AT ALL, IT HAPPENS: A PERFECT FORM EMERGES.

DANIEL LIBESKIND

When I have looked at the site for a building, considered its budget and thought of how it might be built, and what it might be, the drawings come very quickly. I pick up my pen. It flows. A building appears.

OSCAR NIEMEYER

WHEN WE DREW THE ALEXANDRIA LIBRARY, OF COURSE IT WAS BY HAND.

KJETIL TRÆDAL THORSEN

I WOULD LIKE TO REDESIGN PARADISE, BUT I'M NOT IN A GREAT HURRY FOR THAT!

EMILIO AMBASZ

I'VE ALWAYS WANTED TO DO A SCHOOL FOR KIDS. I'M REALLY INTERESTED IN EXPERIENTIAL LEARNING.

TEI CARPENTER

I WANT TO DESIGN SENIOR HOUSING. I'M LOOKING TO MAKE AN IMPACT.

KULAPAT YANTRASAST

I've always wanted to design a house of worship.

DEBORAH BERKE

I WOULD LIKE TO BUILD ON THE SEASHORE.

PETER ZUMTHOR

A football stadium is a dream project. It doesn't make sense to me to spend a billion and a half dollars and use it 12 times a year.

DAVID ROCKWELL

I WANT TO BUILD A CONCERT HALL, AN OPERA HOUSE. I REALLY WANT TO BUILD SOMETHING FOR MUSIC.

PETER MARINO

My dream project would be something that would raise my self-esteem. It would be something that would help me overcome my inner fear.

SLAVA BALBEK

I DREAM OF THE DAY WHEN WE'VE TRULY ACCOMPLISHED A 100 PERCENT CIRCULAR AND CARBON-NEGATIVE PROJECT THROUGH DESIGN EXCELLENCE.

ALEXANDRA HAGEN

THE IDEA OF BUILDING A HOUSE CREATED PURELY BY REMOVING SPACE FROM A MOUNTAIN OF MARBLE, SCULPTING THE VOID WITHIN THE MOUNTAIN, IS A PROJECT I DEFINITELY WANT TO REALIZE BEFORE I DIE.

BJARKE INGELS

I'VE NEVER DONE A HOSPITAL OR A HOTEL OR A TRAIN STATION, BUT I'D BE HAPPY TO DO A SEWAGE SYSTEM IF IT HAD SOME POINT OF DESIGN INTEREST.

JÜRGEN MAYER H.

I READ AN INTERVIEW ONCE WHERE AN ARCHITECT SAID THEIR DREAM JOB WAS TO DO AN AIRPORT. I REMEMBER THINKING THAT WAS NOT HOW I WOULD ANSWER THAT QUESTION.

ANNABELLE SELLDORF

I WOULD LIKE TO DESIGN A WINERY. BECAUSE I LOVE WINE.

SHIGERU BAN

I REMAIN OPEN FOR ALL PROJECTS.

FRANCIS KÉRÉ

I AM TOO SUPERSTITIOUS— I DON'T EVER WISH FOR A PROJECT. I TAKE THE WORK THAT COMES IN THE DOOR AND TRY TO MAKE EACH ONE THE BEST I CAN.

FRANK GEHRY

FASHION

JUMPSUITS ALWAYS— A BRIGHT RED ONE SIGNIFYING ALERT TIME.

KULAPAT YANTRASAST

LEATHER IS MY THING.

PETER MARINO

I WEAR ONLY BLACK, THE ARCHITECTURAL UNIFORM. BUT I'M TRYING TO OPEN MYSELF UP TO A PALETTE BEYOND WHAT I WEAR.

ELIZABETH DILLER

I DON'T SPEND A LOT OF TIME IN SUITS.

GREG LYNN

I like loose clothes with fabrics that flow, hang well, and feel comfortable, as well as having a simple but clear, preferably geometric, structure

SHELLEY MCNAMARA

The last thing I added to my wardrobe was a black fedora by Motsch for Hermès, which was steamed to fit my head perfectly.

JEAN NOUVEL

I HAVE BEEN TRAPPED IN BLACK SINCE I WAS YOUNG.

ODILE DECQ

I DON'T DRESS LIKE A MAVERICK. MY DRESS IS EITHER BROOKS BROTHERS OR J. PRESS.

PETER EISENMAN

THE FUTURE PROJECTS LIGHT, THE PAST ONLY CLOUDS.

EILEEN GRAY

I AM LOOKING FORWARD TO MY OWN SURPRISES.

FRANCIS KÉRÉ

I am incredibly bad at predicting the future; I am only smart enough to observe the present and listen to my intuition about tendencies.

REM KOOLHAAS

WE ONLY CREATE THE PAST; WE NEVER CREATE THE FUTURE BECAUSE THE FUTURE IS NONSENSE. IT DOESN'T EXIST, PERIOD.

PAOLO SOLERI

The future is a journey to the past because maybe the future is not all that is in front of us. It's also what's behind us—the knowledge we had for many centuries, created, adopted, forgotten.

MARIO CUCINELLA

THE FUTURE IS A SPREADING MATRIX RATHER THAN A STRAIGHT LINE. WHAT I AM MAKING NOW CAN BE SEEN AS SEEDS FOR THE FUTURE, ALTHOUGH THOSE SEEDS ARE CREATED BY THE PAST SEEDS OF PAST HISTORIES.

SOU FUJIMOTO

Things we cannot imagine as being in the normal order of events will have happened by tomorrow. Do not be too concerned for today, for today is but the dawn of a new age.

LE CORBUSIER

EVENTUALLY, WE'LL BE MAKING OUR BUILDINGS OUT OF VEGETATION ITSELF.

WINY MAAS

MY LIFE AMBITION IS TO BECOME REDUNDANT, BY TRANSFERRING THE KNOWLEDGE THAT WE HAVE ACQUIRED OR ACCUMULATED TO OTHERS, AND THEN THEY CAN CARRY ON.

YASMEEN LARI

The architects of the future will begin to be seen more as agents of change.

KUNLÉ ADEYEMI

For so long, Native Americans didn't control what our future looked like. Now, there are so many futures to imagine: What do we want our children to see in ten, twenty years? What do we want our grandchildren to see?

SAM OLBEKSON

DESIGNING FOR LONGEVITY ISN'T JUST ABOUT DURABILITY, IT'S ABOUT CREATING PLACES THAT PEOPLE WANT TO RETURN TO.

JEANNE GANG

I PERSONALLY WANT TO CREATE ARCHITECTURE THAT IS "ETERNAL" IN THE SENSE THAT EVEN IF THE BUILDING ITSELF IS WEATHERED AND DECAYED, ITS SCENERY AND SPACE WILL LIVE ON IN THE HEARTS OF THE PEOPLE FOREVER.

TADAO ANDO

WE ARE IN A WORLD WHERE IDEAS ARE SHARED AND MIGRATE. THERE IS NO GOING BACK, SO LET'S GO BEYOND.

FARSHID MOUSSAVI

TODAY IS THE FIRST DAY OF THE FUTURE.

NORMAN FOSTER

We are always concerned about the life of the building after us, and that's probably the more consistent mental attitude that can be seen across all scales of our projects.

PATRICIA VIEL

THE FUTURE IS OUR BIGGEST SECRET.

SÉRGIO BERNARDES

I WAS ALWAYS AN ARCHITECT, NOT A WOMAN ARCHITECT BUT AN ARCHITECT.

ELLAMAE ELLIS LEAGUE

If you google "architect" . . . one of the first images will be a lone white male staring at his sole drawing board.

ELADIA SMOKE

I DIDN'T WANT TO WORK FOR MEN.... I WANTED THE FREEDOM TO EXPLORE MY OWN INTERESTS.

JEANNE GANG

BY 1900, I HAD AN OFFICE "DOWN-TOWN" WITH TWO MEN. THEY LEFT ME HIGH AND DRY AT THE END OF A YEAR—ONE OF THE BEST THINGS THAT EVER HAPPENED TO ME.

LOIS LILLEY HOWE

THE PROFESSION IS NOT MADE IN WOMEN'S IMAGE; BUT AFTER THOUSANDS OF YEARS OF PATRIARCHY THERE IS AN ENORMOUS KNOT TO UNRAVEL....

STEPHANIE MACDONALD

RARELY ARE WOMEN KNOWN AS FEMALE ACCOUNTANTS, FEMALE LAWYERS, FEMALE TAXI DRIVERS, OR FEMALE JOURNALISTS. BUT "FEMALE ARCHITECTS" SEEMS TO BE AN UNSHAKEABLE PHRASE.

DORTE MANDRUP

THE PRIMARY LESSON THAT I HAVE LEARNED IS NOT TO GIVE UP AND TO KEEP GOING, EVEN WHEN IT SEEMS VERY DIFFICULT AND BALANCING EVERYTHING SEEMS IMPOSSIBLE.

CAROLINE BOS

At my age and in my position, I tell other women, "Let's show ourselves. Let's voice ourselves. Let's admit it's not always the easiest."

NATHALIE DE VRIES

WE NEED TO CELEBRATE A RANGE OF WOMEN FROM DIFFERENT PLACES DOING DIFFERENT TYPES OF WORK. OTHERWISE, THE FAMOUS ONES GET INVITED, AND REINVITED, EVERYWHERE.

MADHAVI DESAI

I'VE NEVER HEARD MEN REFERRED TO AS DIFFICULT.

ZAHA HADID

I WAS RECENTLY SITTING IN BUSINESS CLASS ON AN AIRPLANE AND WAS ASKED WHAT I DO BY THE MAN SEATED NEXT TO ME. WHEN I SAID I WAS AN ARCHITECT, HE IMMEDIATELY ASKED, "DO YOU DO INTERIORS?"

DEBORAH BERKE

I AM LOOKING FORWARD TO A TIME WHEN IT IS NOT NECESSARY TO CREATE SEPARATE AWARDS DEDICATED TO WOMEN ARCHITECTS.

MANUELLE GAUTRAND

It’s very interesting to see that women seem to be the braver ones. . . . Whenever I visit disaster areas or work with NGOs there, more than half of the young Japanese architects now are women.

SHIGERU BAN

I WAS TOLD THAT GIRLS DON'T GO TO TECHNICAL UNIVERSITIES.

ITSUKO HASEGAWA

I sometimes go to meetings with a younger male colleague, in which I will ask the questions, and the person I'm addressing will answer my young, male colleague. I find that almost unbelievable, but that still happens.

SARAH WIGGLESWORTH

FIFTY PERCENT
OF MY STUDENTS
ARE FEMALE
AND SOMEHOW
ONLY TWENTY
PERCENT MAKE
IT TO THE
WORKPLACE.

ELIZABETH DILLER

When I started my career, I was coming to many meetings with a lot of men and I was always asked: Oh, can you take notes? I said, No, I am the architect.

ODILE DECQ

IT TOOK A LONG TIME FOR ME TO REALIZE THAT, ACTUALLY, I WAS THE ONE IN THE ROOM WHO KNEW MORE ABOUT A CERTAIN TOPIC THAN ANYBODY ELSE, AND I SHOULD LET THEM KNOW, AND NOT JUST LET THE MEN HOLD THE FLOOR AND PONTIFICATE.

ALISON BROOKS

KNOW THE BARRIERS ARE THERE BUT ACT AS IF THEY ARE NOT.

JULIE EIZENBERG

MY HOUSE IS MY REFUGE, AN EMOTIONAL PIECE OF ARCHITECTURE, NOT A COLD PIECE OF CONVENIENCE.

LUIS BARRAGÁN

If the house doesn't fit you from the soles of your feet to the top of your head it wouldn't be one of our houses.

FRANK LLOYD WRIGHT

THE HOUSE IS A HOME FOR THE SOUL, THE HEART, AND THE SPIRIT. IT IS A CONTAINER FOR THE DAY'S LIGHT, FROM THE PALE YELLOW OF DAWN TO THE DEEP BLUE OF TWILIGHT.

STEVEN HOLL

EACH OF OUR PROJECTS IS NURTURED WITH THE SAME CARE AND ATTACHMENT ONE WOULD DEVOTE TO THEIR OWN CHILD. WE BEGIN WITH BARREN LAND, A CANVAS OF POSSIBILITIES, AND GRADUALLY TRANSFORM IT INTO A HOME.

RAFIQ AZAM

I like the space to look empty, more like a dance floor. My walls are also clear. I do not like hanging pictures on the wall, as it looks way too formal to me.

FRIDA ESCOBEDO

I TRY TO DESIGN HOMES IN WHICH FLEXIBILITY IS A KEY VALUE. MORE SLIDING WALLS THAN DOORS, MORE TRANSPARENCIES THAN WALLS, MORE JOY THAN SOLITUDE.

CINI BOERI

THE HOUSE IS A MACHINE FOR LIVING IN.

LE CORBUSIER

FOR ME THE IDEA OF DESIGNING MY OWN HOUSE IS A NIGHTMARE. WHERE WOULD I BEGIN?

NÍALL MCLAUGHLIN

The home is like a second skin. Whether you have a simple home or a small home, it's a conscious space which affects the way you feel. You shape your home and it shapes you back.

ANUPAMA KUNDOO

At my house, in the heart of Antwerp, it's hard to believe that I'm living in a city. I have an inner courtyard, a wonderful internal garden, a body of water: all the essential elements of nature are there.

VINCENT VAN DUYSEN

I HAVE THIS DREAM WHERE I'LL DESIGN EVERYTHING YOU NEED IN THE HOUSE AS WELL AS THE HOUSE ITSELF.

JOHN PAWSON

A HOUSE IS A LABOR OF LOVE.

EDDIE JONES

HOME IS WHERE AFFECTION RESIDES.

BIJOY JAIN

AMBIGUITY IS A WELCOME TOOL; DOUBT IS ESSENTIAL.

ANNABELLE SELLDORF

DON'T BE AFRAID TO LOOK LIKE YOU DON'T KNOW. YOU ARE NOT MEANT TO KNOW EVERYTHING. EVER. ASK THE QUESTION THAT YOU FEAR MAKES YOU LOOK DUMB. OTHERS WILL BE GRATEFUL, TOO. EVERYONE IS BLUFFING A BIT.

CAMILLA BLOCK

I STILL FEEL LIKE A SHAM—I STILL FEEL LIKE I'VE COBBLED TOGETHER SOMETHING THAT ASPIRES TO BEING A GROWN-UP ARCHITECT.

DAVID CHIPPERFIELD

I FEEL LIKE SUCH AN IMPOSTER. EVERYTHING I DO IS A COLLABORATION, SO I SHOULDN'T BE KNOWN AS THE AUTHOR OF MY WORK.

YASMEEN LARI

I HAVE NEVER CONSIDERED MYSEL[F] A PROFESSIONAL. I HAVE ALWAYS HAD AN OVERWHELMING FEELING OF UNCERTAINTY.

JUHANI PALLASMAA

GO FOR ANY PROJECT THAT PRESENTS AN OPPORTUNITY TO INNOVATE AND NOTHING CAN BE TOO HUMBLE.

NORMAN FOSTER

WE MUST
TRY TO DO THE
BEST WE
CAN, BUT MUST
REMAIN MODEST.
NOTHING
LASTS FOR VERY
LONG.

OSCAR NIEMEYER

To be a good architect actually requires great humility. You have to make the most of the very small amount of knowledge you possess.

SVERRE FEHN

Gone are the days of the 1950s top-down architect dictating how a city should develop. Today, it's about listening—watching how people use space and adapting to how life is, rather than imposing how it should be.

TOSIN OSHINOWO

I like the teachings of our elders: they say we are loving and caring creatures, but sometimes we get sidetracked by our own ego and arrogance.

DOUGLAS CARDINAL

There is no longer a place for the myth of the architect as an individual genius. We inhabit a planet already in decline; ecological maturity demands that architects learn to recognize limits, grieve what is gone, and act with humility.

HARRIET HARRISS

YOU KNOW, I AM STILL TRYING TO THINK OF HOW MANY HOUSES I BUILT AND I DON'T HAVE A CLUE. I NEVER THOUGHT OF COUNTING.

GLENN MURCUTT

DARE TO BE NAÏVE.

BUCKMINSTER FULLER

I HAVE FOUGHT VERY, VERY HARD TO GET PAST BEING KNOWN AS THE MONUMENT MAKER.

MAYA LIN

WHEN I LOOK AT THE WORK ON MY WEBSITE, I THINK TO MYSELF, COULD SOMEONE RECOGNIZE PETER EISENMAN? I AM NOT SURE. I AM NOT BEING DISINGENUOUS. I AM NOT CONVINCED THAT I HAVE A STYLE.

PETER EISENMAN

I've always been a woman. I don't go around thinking of myself as a woman on a daily basis.

ZAHA HADID

I NEVER THOUGHT OF EXPRESSING MYSELF AS AN INDIGENOUS ARCHITECT. I THOUGHT OF EXPRESSING MYSELF AS AN ORGANIC ARCHITECT THAT EMPHASIZED THE BEAUTY AND VITALITY AND RICHNESS OF NATURE.

DOUGLAS CARDINAL

I see myself more as an activist.

SHIGERU BAN

I appreciate both labels of artist and architect, but I know I work in between the two.

YUSSEF AGBO-OLA

Many architects use a strong personal style and form to gain a foothold in the world. No matter where it is, people can tell immediately that it is his or her work with a very strong symbolism. But I am not such a kind of architect.

LIU JIAKUN

I FEEL THAT CHINA IS IN MY BLOOD NO MATTER WHERE I LIVE. CHINA IS MY ROOT.

I. M. PEI

I'M A WANDERER. I'M A LONGTIME SEAMAN, A TRAVELER IN SPIRIT.

BIJOY JAIN

IF THERE IS ONE REAL GREAT PLEASURE IN BECOMING SEVENTY-FIVE YEARS OLD, IT IS THAT YOU ARE ALL HERE TO HELP ME GET OVER THE SHOCK.

WALTER GROPIUS

I HAVE SEVEN CHILDREN AND TEN GRANDCHILDREN AND THREE GREAT-GRANDCHILDREN, SO I MUST BE OLD, BUT I DON'T FEEL OLD, I FEEL YOUNG.

FRANK LLOYD WRIGHT

ALVAR AALTO'S WORK HAS MEANT THE MOST TO ME OF ALL THE WORK OF THE MODERN MASTERS.

ROBERT VENTURI

ONE OF MY GREAT SOURCES HAS BEEN PALLADIO.

CARLO SCARPA

Carlo Scarpa's approach to joints, material transitions, and layered geometries is the hallmark of his architectural style. This influenced me to understand how modernist abstraction can bridge with traditional craft.

DI ZHANG

I was influenced by Joseph Conrad, George Orwell . . . Wendell Berry.

SAMUEL MOCKBEE

I ADMIRE ANTONI GAUDÍ. HE WAS A GENIUS AND AN ADVOCATE FOR NATURE. WITHOUT GAUDÍ, SPANISH ARCHITECTURE IS STILL WONDERFUL, BUT IT WOULD BE LACKING SOMETHING.

MA YANSONG

I was always intrigued by the structural work of Frei Otto, and Buckminster Fuller.

SHIGERU BAN

WHATEVER
I HAVE
LEARNED IN
ARCHITECTURE,
I LEARNED
FROM MY
MOTHER.

RAFIQ AZAM

I DID LIKE KENZŌ TANGE A LOT, BOTH HIS WORK AND AS A PERSON. ONCE I HAD HIM OVER AT A PARTY I HAD AT THE STUDIO. THERE WERE FIREWORKS AND HE WAS JUMPING AROUND WITH DELIGHT.

AGUSTÍN HERNÁNDEZ

EARLY ON, I HAD TWO GREAT MASTERS: AN ARTIST, JOSEPH BEUYS, AND AN ARCHITECT, ALDO ROSSI. WITH THEM I BEGAN TO LAY THE INTELLECTUAL AND FORMAL FOUNDATIONS OF MY ARCHITECTURE.

JACQUES HERZOG

The work of Alessandro Antonelli was certainly among my early enthusiasms for architecture.

ALDO ROSSI

IT'S A BIT OF A CLICHÉ THAT RENAISSANCE ARCHITECTURE MADE ME REALIZE WHAT I WANTED TO DO, BUT IT'S REALLY TRUE.

TOSHIKO MORI

I THINK WE ARE ALL THE SUBJECT OF INFLUENCES. SOME OF THOSE INFLUENCES WE IMMEDIATELY IDENTIFY. WE REFER TO THEM. OTHERS ARE MORE SUBCONSCIOUS.

NORMAN FOSTER

I THINK LE CORBUSIER IS PROBABLY THE ABSOLUTE MASTER IN TERMS OF HOW WE DEFINE MODERNITY TODAY. WE ARE STILL FOLLOWING HIM AS A MODEL OF ARCHITECTURE. . . .

PATRICIA VIEL

Le Corbusier, the genius, most versatile, like Leonardo da Vinci or Picasso, has not built much. But in sketches and indications he has opened up the most new worlds.

EERO SAARINEN

AUGUSTE PERRET OCCUPIES A VERY HIGH, A VERY DEFINITE PLACE IN THE HISTORY OF MODERN ARCHITECTURE; FOR HE WAS A "CONSTRUCTOR."

LE CORBUSIER

LE CORBUSIER, MIES VAN DER ROHE, OSCAR NIEMEYER. THESE ARE AN UNFORGETTABLE "TRIO" FOR ME.

RYUE NISHIZAWA

THE PERSON I ALWAYS CONNECTED WITH, BUT NEVER MET, WAS THE BRAZILIAN ARCHITECT LINA BO BARDI. HER WORK SPOKE TO ME.

JEANNE GANG

THE NEW YORK GUGGENHEIM HAS HAD AN INCREDIBLE INFLUENCE ON ME.

ZAHA HADID

ONE OF MY STRONGEST INFLUENCES WAS THE SCULPTOR ISAMU NOGUCHI.

TADAO ANDO

AT ARCHITECTURE SCHOOL I HAD ALEJANDRO DE LA SOTA AS [A] TEACHER, AND WHEN I MET HIM, I THOUGHT, "I WANT TO BE LIKE HIM."

ALBERTO CAMPO BAEZA

THE ARCHITECTURE OF NIEMEYER KNOWS NO LIMITS. THE BEAUTY, THE POWER OF IT HAS NO LIMITS.

FRANCIS KÉRÉ

I WANT TO BE LIKE OSCAR NIEMEYER WHO, DYING IN A HOSPITAL BED IN RIO DE JANEIRO AT THE AGE OF 104, WAS WORRIED ABOUT NOT GETTING BACK TO HIS OFFICE BECAUSE HE STILL HAD SOME PROJECTS TO FINISH.

MARCIO KOGAN

A SUNSET AND A PRAYER SERMON SIT ON THE SAME PLANE OF INSPIRATION FOR ME.

SUMAYYA VALLY

FOR ME, EVERYTHING I LIVE AND EXPERIENCE FILTERS THROUGH INTO MY WORK.

FRIDA ESCOBEDO

When I was eighteen and ready to go to university my father sent me to see Le Corbusier's Monastery of Sainte Marie de La Tourette near Lyon, France. . . . When I saw the monastery's chapel, I was speechless. I decided—if this is architecture—I want to be an architect.

WOLF PRIX

I still remember the emotion I felt when I first saw the Reichstag in Berlin being wrapped by Christo: thousands of people were singing and dancing, they flocked to see the building being wrapped up. . . . That day I fully understood for the first time that the world is fascinated by fantastic projects.

ZAHA HADID

I am always in awe of engineering feats, so the Pantheon stands out as a favorite. The endurance and scale of that structure is amazing, but the poetry of its spatial connection to the sky makes it deeply architectural.

JEANNE GANG

I AM
MUCH
MORE
INSPIRED
BY THE
OTHER ARTS
THAN
ARCHITECTURE.

ISAY WEINFELD

Often when our son was young, we would spend a huge amount of time at the Museum of Natural History in New York. There are very many inspiring ideas there, or things you would see, that would come back into our work.

BILLIE TSIEN

WHEN I WAS A TEENAGER, I LOVED THE WORK OF THOMAS HARDY, THE ENGLISH WRITER.

YVONNE FARRELL

WHEN BEGINNING A NEW PROJECT, I HAVE PRACTICALLY NEVER LOOKED AT PROJECTS OF OTHER ARCHITECTS IN SIMILAR TASKS. I MOSTLY LOOK AT PAINTINGS. . . .

JUHANI PALLASMAA

I HAVE RECENTLY DISCOVERED THE WORK OF WISŁAWA SZYMBORSKA, A POLISH POET THAT I FIND PARTICULARLY STIRRING.

CARLA JUAÇABA

When I look at Isamu Noguchi's lighting fixtures, I'm still blown away by them, and I think, "It would be hard to surpass these."

KEIJI ASHIZAWA

I LIKE MONUMENTAL ARCHITECTURE. I'M PRO THINGS THAT WERE BUILT A LONG TIME AGO—FOR EXAMPLE, THE PYRAMIDS.

SLAVA BALBEK

I HAVE UNDENIABLY BEEN VERY INSPIRED BY PRE-HISPANIC FORMS—NOT JUST ARCHITECTURALLY SPEAKING, EVEN THE URBANISM OF ANCIENT MEXICO IS A SOURCE OF WONDERMENT TO ME.

AGUSTÍN HERNÁNDEZ

The lessons learned from the unassuming architecture of our Mexican provincial towns have been a permanent source of inspiration. The white-washed walls, the solitude of patios and orchards, the colorful walls of houses in the streets. . . .

LUIS BARRAGÁN

THERE IS NOTHING MORE SOPHISTICATED—SCIENTIFICALLY, TECHNICALLY—THAN A FLOWER. THE WAY IT OPENS AND CLOSES, IT IS MAGICAL, AND IN OUR GARDEN, IT IS REPEATED THOUSANDS OF TIMES.

SANTIAGO CALATRAVA

I like the idea of learning from others. My wife, Susan, and I have a working farm on Bruny Island in Tasmania that produces wool. There is a lot that we can learn from farmers.

JOHN WARDLE

I LOVE TO PEOPLE-WATCH SO MY IDEAL PERIODS OF INSPIRATION COME FROM WATCHING PEOPLE INTERACT WITH SPACE.

TOSIN OSHINOWO

THE SUN NEVER KNEW HOW GREAT IT WAS UNTIL IT STRUCK THE SIDE OF A BUILDING.

LOUIS KAHN

ONE CAN CREATE ARCHITECTURE SIMPLY BY PURSUING LIGHT.

TADAO ANDO

NATURAL LIGHT IS ONE OF THE MOST IMPORTANT ELEMENTS IN MY WORK. NOT ONLY DOES IT ALLOW US TO CONNECT WITH THE ENVIRONMENT VISUALLY, BUT IT ALSO SHOWS THE PASSAGE OF TIME.

KENGO KUMA

I have always been interested in how light hits buildings and in capturing a very painterly "brushstroke" in my buildings.

FRANK GEHRY

LIGHT DOESN'T JUST ILLUMINATE; IT SCULPTS THE EXPERIENCE OF BEING IN THE SPACE.

JORIS POGGIOLI

ONE OF THE CONSTANT ELEMENTS OF MY INSPIRATION IS LIGHT. MAYBE THIS COMES FROM THE FACT THAT I'M FROM THE CITY OF LIGHT THAT IS GENOA, ON THE WATER.

RENZO PIANO

WE CHASE THE SUN HERE IN DENMARK BECAUSE IT IS SO PRECIOUS.

DAVID THULSTRUP

BEDROOMS AND LIBRARIES OUGHT TO HAVE AN EASTERN EXPOSURE, BECAUSE THEIR PURPOSES REQUIRE THE MORNING LIGHT, AND ALSO BECAUSE BOOKS IN SUCH LIBRARIES WILL NOT DECAY.

VITRUVIUS

Light is the "clue" material to achieve any kind of ambience, while darkness offers you another perception of the space. I believe a designer must use light the same way as the sunlight falls on buildings—in a continuous play between the filters, reflections, and itself.

RAFAEL ARANDA

IN MY ARCHITECTURE IT'S ALWAYS A BALANCE BETWEEN SPACES THAT ARE BATHED IN LIGHT, COMPLEMENTED BY SPACES THAT ARE DARKER, MORE SUBDUED, AND CALMING.

VINCENT VAN DUYSEN

WITHOUT LIGHT, WE DO NOT HAVE ARCHITECTURE.

RICK JOY

WORKING WITH WOOD FOR SO MANY YEARS IN MY PRACTICE, IT'S BECOME ALMOST LIKE A FRIEND TO ME. I UNDERSTAND IT.

KENGO KUMA

ADOLF LOOS, THE GREAT ARCHITECT, ONCE SAID, "IF YOU GAVE ME GOLD, I WOULD STILL USE WOOD." I IDENTIFY WITH THAT.

DANIEL LIBESKIND

An architect must be able to understand the structure of the tree, the heaviness and hardness of the stone, the character of glass; he must become one with his materials and be able to form and use them in harmony with their nature.

JØRN UTZON

[TREES] HAVE A LIFE OF THEIR OWN, AND YOU FEEL A DEEP RESPECT FOR THE TIME IT HAS TAKEN TO GROW. WE WORK WITH SOMETHING ALIVE, AN ORGANIC MATERIAL. WE CAN'T DO AS WE PLEASE WITH IT. . . .

SIV HELENE STANGELAND

We have to accept that not everyone appreciates concrete as a finished material the way we do.

TATIANA BILBAO

I LOVE THE STONE OF PARIS. IT'S LIKE THE STUCCO OF LA.

FRANK GEHRY

We started working with simpler materials because we were a small firm. At one point, it was just me in my kitchen. I had to learn to work with simple means, and that meant using cinder blocks or things perceived as very cheap.

FRIDA ESCOBEDO

PASSION CAN CREATE DRAMA OUT OF INERT STONE.

LE CORBUSIER

I GREW UP WITH STEEL. I'M VERY COMFORTABLE WITH STEEL. THAT OBVIOUSLY HAD A HUGE EFFECT ON MY CAREER.

TOM KUNDIG

I always try to use materials in my work that never have to be painted.

ALISON BROOKS

I ALWAYS USE THE MATERIALS RATHER THAN THE FORMS IN ORDER TO GIVE EXPRESSION TO A BUILDING. I ALWAYS SAY, "ARCHITECTURE IS THE 'MATERIALIZATION' OF A CONCEPT."

BERNARD TSCHUMI

WE CONSIDER COLOR TO BE A BUILDING MATERIAL JUST LIKE CONCRETE OR BRICK.

LOUISA HUTTON

I AM MORE INTERESTED IN GEOMETRY THAT WILL FORCE ME TO DO THINGS WITH MATERIALS I HAVE, THAN TO FORECAST AND INVENT AN IDEAL MATERIAL FOR SOMETHING NOT PLANNED YET.

CECIL BALMOND

MY WORKS USE VERY ORDINARY MATERIALS. THEY ARE BUILT WITH CONCRETE, THEY ARE BUILT WITH STEEL, SOMETIMES WE PAVE THINGS WITH STONE OR EVEN WITH ASPHALT. THESE ARE PLACES THAT HUNDREDS, EVEN THOUSANDS, OF PEOPLE GO THROUGH AND THE STRUCTURES NEED TO INCORPORATE VERY RESILIENT AND ROUGH-WEARING MATERIALS.

SANTIAGO CALATRAVA

I WORK WITH MUD.

YASMEEN LARI

IN A SENSE, LIGHT ITSELF IS LIKE THE EXTREME, IDEAL MATERIAL FOR ARCHITECTS.

SOU FUJIMOTO

MY FAVORITE MATERIAL IS LIGHT.

STEVEN HOLL

BAMBOO IS THE GREEN STEEL OF THE TWENTY-FIRST CENTURY.

VO TRONG NGHIA

Using a material that is ubiquitous, that is everywhere, but still creating something that nobody else can—that's my motto.

TADAO ANDO

IF DESIGNED AND INSTALLED CORRECTLY, AN ALUMINUM STRUCTURE CAN BE AS STRONG AS A STEEL ONE. I BECAME INTERESTED IN ALUMINUM AS A STRUCTURAL MATERIAL BECAUSE IT WASN'T BEING USED IN THIS WAY.

RIKEN YAMAMOTO

Aluminum is a beautiful material. It has brought to exteriors a new color, a color that did not previously exist for them—silver. When properly anodized it looks like velvet.

GIO PONTI

Glass technology is highly advanced, but the product still remains extremely mysterious today; it is therefore important to continue to experiment with it.

BENEDETTA TAGLIABUE

Glass is one of the most fantastic materials; it can even be bent at right angles.

RENZO PIANO

Any work of architecture which does not express serenity is a mistake. That is why it has been an error to replace the protection of walls with today's intemperate use of enormous glass windows.

LUIS BARRAGÁN

IF YOU TALK TO A BRICK AND ASK IT WHAT IT LIKES, IT'LL SAY IT LIKES AN ARCH.

LOUIS KAHN

Brick has a special richness: out of a single module in three dimensions, you have an infinity of possibilities. The future should be going back to the basics and discovering that infinity.

OLIVIER MARTY

BRICKS WILL BE MOST SERVICEABLE IF MADE TWO YEARS BEFORE USING; FOR THEY CANNOT DRY THOROUGHLY IN LESS TIME.

VITRUVIUS

I APPRECIATE THE SENSUAL QUALITY OF ARCHITECTURE AND THE TEXTURE OF THE MATERIAL.

ODILE DECQ

Sense emerges when I succeed in bringing out the specific meanings of certain materials in my buildings, meanings that can only be perceived in just this way in this one building.

PETER ZUMTHOR

I AM OBSESSED WITH MATERIAL CONTRAST. IT IS SO IMPORTANT TO HAVE THE RIGHT BALANCE OF RAW AND SLEEK; OLD AND NEW.

DAVID THULSTRUP

GROWN, CAST, CUT, OR MOLDED MATERIALS THAT AGE HAVE A DEPTH THAT CAN SUSTAIN OUR IMAGINATION. THEY CONTAIN WORLDS YOU CANNOT SUBSTITUTE. THEY ALSO CARRY A LOT OF REFERENCE AND CULTURAL CONTENT.

STEPHANIE MACDONALD

Regardless of what material we're using, we try to use it with respect so that it maintains its dignity and that it doesn't become sanitized by virtue of mass production.

SHELLEY MCNAMARA

Timber is a wonderful material. The tree, with its hierarchy of parts and capacity for yielding dimensional variation, inspires ways of building as diverse as weaving with fibers.

BRIT ANDRESEN

One of the few sustainable materials is timber. Steel and aluminum require much more energy to produce. They should be used sparingly.

GLENN MURCUTT

I particularly like steel, but paper too can be strong and permanent. We need to get rid of material prejudices.

SHIGERU BAN

From my own heritage of the Indigenous ethnic groups of Yoruba and Cherokee lineage there is a deep cultural understanding that all materials have a living energy within them and that matter has a profound memory or sacredness.

YUSSEF AGBO-OLA

WHEN I SEE WOOD, I ALSO SEE THE TREE—AND THE FOREST.

BRINDA SOMAYA

WE ACTUALLY THINK OF TIME AS A MATERIAL IN OUR WORK.

BRIGITTE SHIM

I WANT TO HAVE MY OWN BRONZE FOUNDRY SOON, SO I CAN WORK IN BRONZE BECAUSE I WANT TO WORK WITH FIRE AS A MATERIAL IN MUMBAI.

BIJOY JAIN

I really love the idea of water as a collaborator. It’s this element that you can’t tame. Water is alive, it’s dynamic, it’s moving, and it has different material states.

TEI CARPENTER

THE EXISTING BUILDING IS TOMORROW'S NEW BUILDING MATERIAL.

ANNE LACATON

THE IMPORTANCE OF A PROJECT HAS NOTHING TO DO WITH THE BUDGET.

SHIGERU BAN

If somebody comes in and says, "Can you build a shack for $10?" I might take that just as easily as a grandiose project in the center of Paris. Because I come from a working-class background, I never thought architecture should be about how much money you have.

DANIEL LIBESKIND

Luxury is light, air, space. It is not about the expensive kitchen or imported woods. It is about understanding the quality of shade or a tree. And that can be accessible to all.

FERNANDA CANALES

WE NEVER COUNTED HOW MANY HOURS WE WORKED FOR ANY PROJECT. WE MAY HAVE LOST IT IN SOME AND GAINED IT IN OTHERS. I WOULD SAY THAT WE WERE FINANCIALLY SUCCESSFUL BY NOT THINKING ABOUT FINANCIAL SUCCESS.

FARSHID MOUSSAVI

WE WORKED EVERY DAY, EVERY NIGHT. WE WORKED SATURDAY. WE WORKED SUNDAY. WE WORKED HOLIDAYS—EVERYTHING. WE GOT $25 A WEEK. THAT WAS GOOD MONEY.

NATALIE DE BLOIS

I find myself for the moment very hard up and I was wondering if you could see your way to buy one of my flower pictures or landscapes . . . as my rent of 16 pounds is overdue and I must pay or leave.

CHARLES RENNIE MACKINTOSH

I HATE TO ASK FOR MONEY ALWAYS, BUT WHAT CAN I DO?

FRANK LLOYD WRIGHT

I CAN'T HELP BUT FEEL THAT A SYSTEM WHERE THE FOCUS IS ON BUDGET RATHER THAN ON THE ESSENCE OF ARCHITECTURE IS NOT A HEALTHY ONE.

TSUYOSHI TANE

I DON'T GIVE A FUCK IF WE'RE ON BUDGET.

PETER ZUMTHOR

THE MEETING PLACE FOR A COMMUNITY SHOULD NOT BE ABOUT MONEY, IT'S ABOUT SOMETHING MUCH MORE IMPORTANT, MUCH MORE SIGNIFICANT, MUCH DEEPER THAN THAT.

AMANDA LEVETE

The biggest challenge was learning how to negotiate fees. . . . I was constantly negotiated down with the tactic of seeing "the opportunity of completing the project."

TOSIN OSHINOWO

WE'RE TRYING TO DO AS MUCH AS POSSIBLE WITH AS LITTLE AS POSSIBLE WHILE ALSO REDUCING AS MUCH AS POSSIBLE THE DEBT OF THE PEOPLE WHO ARE ACQUIRING THESE PROPERTIES.

FRIDA ESCOBEDO

THE LINE BETWEEN PROFESSIONAL HONESTY AND FINANCIAL EXPEDIENCY IS FINE AND WE SPEND MOST OF THE TIME ON THE WRONG SIDE OF IT.

RICHARD ROGERS

I'M SCARED STIFF OF PEOPLE WHO LOOK AT THINGS FROM THE MONEY ANGLE.

LOUIS KAHN

MUSEUMS

A WHITE BOX KILLS ART.

RENZO PIANO

WHAT I LOVE ABOUT WORKING IN MUSEUMS, WITH ART AND CURATORS AND DIRECTORS, IS THAT THE DIALOGUE IS VERY INTIMATE. THE WAY TO GAIN PERSPECTIVE IS TO REALLY UNDERSTAND WHAT MATTERS TO THEM.

ANNABELLE SELLDORF

WHEN I DESIGN SPACES FOR ART, I THINK OF MYSELF AS A KEEN MATCH-MAKER BETWEEN ART AND PEOPLE— LIKE TWO GOOD FRIENDS THAT YOU WANT TO SET UP.

KULAPAT YANTRASAST

In museums, it's not only a question of how you exhibit the art, but also about how, through complexity, curators can interpret different leads and different connections.

ZAHA HADID

DESIGNING FOR ART DEMANDS HUMILITY. THESE ARE SPACES OF ENCOUNTER, BETWEEN ARTWORKS, VIEWERS, AND TIME ITSELF. ARCHITECTURE MUST OFFER SILENCE AND PRESENCE AT ONCE.

LINA GHOTMEH

A museum building certainly has to be more than a mere receptacle for collections. We expect it to satisfy higher demands, to have what we call a "monumental" expression and, as such, to embody the civic and cultural pride of the community.

WALTER GROPIUS

A museum building should be like a city. It's boring to immediately understand everything. But it should not be impossible to understand, either. Every time you go back, you should get to know it a little better.

KAZUYO SEJIMA

I think the best museums are those that are free. You go there for maybe ten minutes, see something, and leave. It's like walking through a park. You see a beautiful tree, a dog jumping, and then you move on.

SMILJAN RADIĆ

SOMEBODY SAID THAT THE MUSEUM OUT HERE ON FIFTH AVENUE [THE GUGGENHEIM] LOOKED LIKE A WASHING MACHINE. . . . I'VE HEARD A LOT OF THAT TYPE OF REACTION AND I'VE ALWAYS DISCOUNTED IT AS WORTHLESS, AND I THINK IT IS.

FRANK LLOYD WRIGHT

SOON AFTER I FINISHED BILBAO, THE DIRECTOR OF AN LA MUSEUM TOLD ME HE HAD ATTENDED A PROFESSIONAL CONFERENCE WHERE A RESOLUTION WAS PASSED TO NOT LET ME DO ANOTHER MUSEUM, EVER.

FRANK GEHRY

A MUSEUM— A BUILDING IN GENERAL— IS NEVER FINISHED.

PIERRE DE MEURON

HUMANS SEEM TO KNOW MORE ABOUT LIVING ON THE MOON THAN LIVING ON THE OCEAN. THIS NEEDS TO CHANGE.

KUNLÉ ADEYEMI

THERE IS NOTHING MORE PLEASANT THAN SITTING IN THE SHADE OF A TREE WITH A GENTLE BREEZE AND LIGHT FILTERING THROUGH THE LEAVES. IN JAPAN, THIS IS CALLED KOMOREBI. AS ARCHITECTS, WE CAN DESIGN SPACES LIKE THIS.

WAEL AL AWAR

In each house, I design a green room to contemplate nature, a wind room for the hot season, and a rain room to listen to the melody of the rain.

RAFIQ AZAM

When I started professionally as an architect, I passionately believed that if you had a shaft of sunlight, if you had a view, then you were going to be happier. The difference now is that it has been scientifically proven.

NORMAN FOSTER

WITHOUT NATURE AROUND US WE BECOME CRAZY.

VO TRONG NGHIA

More and more I believe we are climate beings, linked to our geography, the soil, topography, weather, and what we eat.

LINA GHOTMEH

IF I AM ANXIOUS FOR SOME REASON, EVERYTHING SETTLES DOWN BY GOING TO THE FOREST FOR A HALF AN HOUR.

JUHANI PALLASMAA

THE BIGGEST DEBATE BETWEEN NATIVE CULTURES AND THE WESTERN WORLD, IS THAT FOR NATIVE CULTURES, NATURE IS A BEING. AND THAT BEING HAS TO BE UNDERSTOOD. . . . FOR THE WESTERN WORLD, NATURE IS A THING. AS A THING, YOU CAN OPERATE OVER NATURE.

ALEJANDRO ARAVENA

EVERYTHING MAN IS DOING IN ARCHITECTURE IS TO TRY TO GO AGAINST NATURE. THE IDEA TO BE A PART OF NATURE IS A BRAND NEW IDEA OF THE LAST CENTURY.

FREI OTTO

IT IS NOT ABOUT TIPTOEING ON THE EARTH. IT IS ABOUT BEING EMBEDDED IN IT AND LOVING IT.

CAMILLA BLOCK

What about human resourcefulness? The scarcity narrative deprives the next generation instead of giving them a head start. We are only “depleting our natural resources” because of how we use and think about them.

ANUPAMA KUNDOO

I LOVE THE EASTERN MEADOWLARK. I ALWAYS HAVE.

MAYA LIN

Because I was from the countryside, playing in the forest and being immersed in nature was quite an important starting point to form my perception of space. In a natural environment, you can choose your own path.

SOU FUJIMOTO

NO MATTER HOW BIG YOU THINK YOUR BUILDING IS, IT'S PUNY IN RELATION TO THE LANDSCAPE.

BRIGITTE SHIM

I WATCHED A SPIDER BUILD A WEB, AND I THOUGHT MY GOODNESS THAT'S MY SOLUTION FOR THE ROOF!

DOUGLAS CARDINAL

IT IS ALL ABOUT HOW HUMAN BEINGS PERCEIVE AND VIEW NATURE. WE DON'T OWN IT—WE ARE PART OF IT.

MA YANSONG

I UNDERSTAND THAT MY BUILDINGS ARE NOT NATURE, BUT I WOULD LOVE IF THEY BECAME PART OF IT IN A WAY.

PETER ZUMTHOR

PHILOSOPHY

FORM EVER FOLLOWS FUNCTION.

LOUIS SULLIVAN

THERE IS NO ARCHITECTURE WITHOUT A PHILOSOPHY. THERE IS NO ART OF ANY KIND WITHOUT ITS OWN PHILOSOPHY.

FRANK LLOYD WRIGHT

EVERY REALLY GOOD ARCHITECT DEVELOPS—EITHER VISUALLY OR VERBALLY OR BOTH—A COHERENT WORLDVIEW.

LEBBEUS WOODS

WE'RE NOT PRESERVATIONISTS. WE DON'T BELIEVE IN MUMMIFYING OLD STRUCTURES. WE DO BELIEVE IN BREATHING LIFE INTO OLD THINGS WHERE WE CAN.

ELIZABETH DILLER

I think the word "reinvention" is the key word of today. . . . It's a word that I have always cherished, more than "invention."

REM KOOLHAAS

I believe that if people love their environment, they take better care of it.

SOU FUJIMOTO

I BELIEVE SO MUCH IN THE POWER OF BEGINNING.

LOUIS KAHN

We give the same importance to a master plan as we do to a doorknob.

MARCIO KOGAN

MY WIFE'S PHILOSOPHY, VIEWING EVERY HOUR SPENT IN DISAGREEMENT AS AN HOUR LOST, HAS RESHAPED MY OUTLOOK ON LIFE AND WORK.

RAFIQ AZAM

I try through my work to locate human beings in a more authentic relationship to the environment and to each other

MPHETHI MOROJELE

LET'S NOT PRODUCE A HERITAGE OF JUNK FOR THE NEXT GENERATION, BUT A HERITAGE OF BEAUTY AND A HERITAGE OF CREATIVITY AND A HERITAGE OF BELONGING ON THIS BEAUTIFUL PLANET.

DOUGLAS CARDINAL

I FIRMLY BELIEVE THAT A BUILDING THAT IS BUILT WITH LOVE EMANATES A CERTAIN ENERGY.

RICHARD ENGLAND

I WANT TO MAKE ARCHITECTURE THAT ALLOWS PEOPLE TO BE RELAXED—TO BE EATING AND READING WHILE LYING DOWN, WHICH IS GETTING CLOSER TO A NATURAL CONDITION.

TOYO ITO

A BUILDING THAT RELATES TO ELEMENTS SUCH AS LIGHT, OPENINGS, AND COLOR OF MATERIALITY GIVES MORE TO A LITTLE CHILD THAN A ROOM WHERE YOU CAN TEACH THE ALPHABET. THIS ROOM IS GIVING THESE YOUNG KIDS INSPIRATION

FRANCIS KÉRÉ

I believe that architecture necessarily has to have an aspect of political expression. What the Pantheon made so impressively clear was that space did not belong to the individual and was something for everybody to experience together.

RYUE NISHIZAWA

Buildings are knowledge carriers. They remember things that we forget. And as long as we spend a little time with them, and we listen to them and decipher their language, they will speak to us.

LISA LANDRUM

WE BELIEVE THE PROJECT NEEDS TO HAVE A SOUL; IT NEEDS TO HAVE A BEAUTY, A CALM AND SERENITY. THE "SOUL" IS SOMETHING WE CONSIDER EXTREMELY IMPORTANT IN THE ARCHITECTURE THAT WE DELIVER.

RAFAEL ARANDA

Humanism is probably the thing that connects all our projects.

MICHAEL GRAVES

A GOOD DESIGN IS MODEST, HAS A LONG LIFE, AND WORKS IN ANY SITUATION.

KEIJI ASHIZAWA

It's important that our projects create a new social life for the location. Design must help people to evolve their lives.

SEYHAN ÖZDEMIR

I DON'T NEED A MANIFESTO. I HAVE A VERY ORDINARY ATTITUDE IN LIFE, WHICH IS TO DO ORDINARY THINGS EXTRAORDINARILY WELL.

GLENN MURCUTT

QUESTIONS

THERE ARE 360 DEGREES, SO WHY STICK TO ONE?

ZAHA HADID

TO ME, ARCHITECTURE IS A KIND OF HYPOTHESIS. YOU ARE POSING QUESTIONS. EVERY PROJECT IS AN EXPERIMENT.

CECIL BALMOND

We just keep coming back and asking questions and trying to figure out what the right questions are to ask until we exhaust ourselves.

ANDREW FREEAR

TO CREATE, ONE MUST FIRST QUESTION EVERYTHING.

EILEEN GRAY

Practicing architecture is asking oneself questions, finding one's own answers with the help of the teacher, whittling down, finding solutions. Over and over again.

PETER ZUMTHOR

How can I design so that tens of thousands of people feel comfortable?

FRANCIS KÉRÉ

With the increasing world population from 7.5 billion to 10 billion by 2050, we have to house two-point something billion people in the next thirty-five to forty years. How will we do that?

WAEL AL AWAR

IF YOU WALK DOWN THE STREET AND SEE THE PEOPLE, DON'T YOU IMMEDIATELY FEEL, "WHAT CAN I DO FOR THEM?"

BALKRISHNA DOSHI

WHY SHOULD WE ONLY ACT WHEN A DISASTER OCCURS? WHY CAN'T WE DO SOMETHING BEFORE?

YASMEEN LARI

What if architects could participate in policymaking and not simply follow it? Could this be considered architectural design as well?

FRIDA ESCOBEDO

I DON'T THINK YOU NEED SUPER-TALL BUILDINGS.

PETER EISENMAN

What is the chief characteristic of the tall office building? . . . It must be tall, every inch of it tall. The force and power of altitude must be in it, the glory and pride of exaltation must be in it. It must be every inch a proud and soaring thing, rising in sheer exultation that from bottom to top it is a unit without a single dissenting line. . . .

LOUIS SULLIVAN

WHAT IS DONE IN ALL THE OFFICE DISTRICTS IS NO LONGER TOWERS, IT'S JUST HIGH CAGES.

JEAN NOUVEL

I DON'T THINK THERE'S ANYTHING CRIMINAL ABOUT HAVING A VERY, VERY SMALL APARTMENT, LIKE A SHIP'S CABIN WITH EVERYTHING BUILT IN.

NICHOLAS GRIMSHAW

People can be surprised that I jump between scales, and sometimes I do houses that are so small, they can fit into a single room of another house I have designed in the past. But for me, the priorities remain the same. It is about simple materials, natural light, cross ventilation, and creating a safe space.

FERNANDA CANALES

Small rooms or dwellings set the mind in the right path, large ones cause it to go astray.

LEONARDO DA VINCI

Small-scale means you can make it happen faster. It's realistic. It's pragmatism. . . . This way you also value local capacity and resources, which in turn contributes to the local economy. This is the power we need to seek! It's small, but it's strong!

FRANCIS KÉRÉ

We would love to jump from 1,000 units of social housing to a million units. Maybe someone else can find a way to make the leap in scale.

ALEJANDRO ARAVENA

It has been said that were I three inches taller than 5' 8½" all my houses would have been quite different in proportion. Probably.

FRANK LLOYD WRIGHT

In our office, we're proud of the very small things we do. Could be a piece of jewelry, or cutlery. . . . The scale is very exciting for us, we're able to do every scale.

ZAHA HADID

I'm as happy designing an outhouse if it has potential as I am doing very complicated projects.

EDDIE JONES

WHY SMALL AND LARGE ROOMS? BECAUSE ONE DOES NOT SPEAK IN THE SAME WAY IN A SMALL ROOM AS IN A LARGE ONE.

LOUIS KAHN

WE'RE NOT ONLY THINKING FROM OUTSIDE IN ON THESE BUILDINGS, BUT ALSO FROM INSIDE OUT. WE COME AT IT FROM THE SCALE OF THE LIVING SPACE, THEN THE SCALE OF THE SOCIAL SPACE, AND THE SCALE WITHIN THE CITY.

JEANNE GANG

IDEAS CAN MIGRATE FROM SCALE TO SCALE.

JOHN WARDLE

I LIKE TO THINK OF SUSTAINABILITY IN TERMS OF "SUSTAINING PEOPLE."

MARIAM ISSOUFOU

WE HAVE ABUNDANCE. WE JUST NEED TO LEARN HOW TO USE IT. THAT'S WHAT HUMANS HAVE DONE FOR CENTURIES.

ANUPAMA KUNDOO

WE HAVE MOVED BEYOND THE POINT OF "ZERO IMPACT." WE REALLY SHOULD BE TALKING ABOUT REGENERATION AND RENEWAL, NOT SUSTAINABILITY. ZERO IMPACT IS NOT ENOUGH, CONSIDERING WHAT WE'VE DONE SO FAR.

TOSIN OSHINOWO

TO REKINDLE OUR DAMAGED RELATIONSHIP WITH NATURE, WE MUST DESIGN ALONGSIDE HER AND BE MORE MINDFUL OF HOW OUR WORK AFFECTS HER.

MARIO CUCINELLA

Sustainability is not a theoretical concept or an added feature for enhancing business. It's a holistic way of designing and building, a system that involves participation and thinking.

SALMA SAMAR DAMLUJI

TO HAVE CONTROL OVER THE SUSTAINABILITY OF AN ARCHITECTURAL PROJECT, TODAY YOU NO LONGER HAVE TO THINK OF ARCHITECTURE FROM A GEOMETRIC POINT OF VIEW, BUT YOU HAVE TO SOMEHOW DESIGN THE BEHAVIOR.

PATRICIA VIEL

FOR DECADES, PEOPLE HAVE BELIEVED THAT THE OLD IS BAD COMPARED TO WHAT IS NEW, AND THAT REUSE AND RENOVATION ARE MORE EXPENSIVE. . . . YOU CAN'T ERASE EVERYTHING THAT EXISTS AND BE SUSTAINABLE.

ANNE LACATON

Not every building can or should be preserved in its entirety, but they each represent carbon that has already been released. Taking them down would mean expending more carbon to replace them. For this reason, we must use as much as we can of what's already there going forward.

JEANNE GANG

THERE IS NOTHING NEW ABOUT SUSTAINABLE MATERIALS, AS WE HAVE ALREADY BEEN USING THEM FOR A LONG TIME.

BENEDETTA TAGLIABUE

The term "sustainability" quickly became a bit hollow for us. . . . We preferred to use the term "attainability"— a combination of affordability and sustainability.

CAROLINE BOS

The definitions of greenness, of politically correct materials for ecology considerations, are completely different depending on who's building the material, how it's being built, what the effects are in the community, and how far it needs to travel to get to the construction site.

FERNANDA CANALES

We think—whatever one's various preoccupations are—that our generation will be measured by the sustainability of what we leave behind to an increasingly overpopulated planet.

LOUISA HUTTON

We are moving from an egocentric society to an ecocentric one, in which the human being is not the tip of the pyramid, but is part of a complex system of relationships.

CAZÚ ZEGERS

We should always first think: Do I really need to demolish?

JACOB VAN RIJS

If we design buildings really well, the chance of them having to be redeveloped is reduced. And the important thing about the longevity of the building is that it is worth keeping. If it's worth keeping, then you have the beginning of sustainability in a true sense.

GLENN MURCUTT

EVENTUALLY EVERY SINGLE ONE OF US WILL HAVE TO RESPOND TO HIS OR HER CONSCIENCE. WILL WE BE MAKERS OR BREAKERS OF A SUSTAINABLE CIVILIZATION ON OUR PLANET?

PAOLO SOLERI

SUSTAINABILITY IN THE END IS NOTHING BUT THE RIGOROUS USE OF COMMON SENSE.

ALEJANDRO ARAVENA

OUR OFFICE ACTS LIKE A KIND OF EDUCATIONAL ESTABLISHMENT AND WE ARE VERY CAREFUL WHO WE EDUCATE.

REM KOOLHAAS

I FEEL THAT BEING IN SCHOOL IS LIKE BEING IN A CHAPEL, AND MY DUTY IS TO WRITE PSALMS. I COME MUCH MORE REFRESHED AND CHALLENGED FROM THE CLASSES. I LEARN MORE FROM THE STUDENTS THAN I PROBABLY TEACH.

LOUIS KAHN

No little kid goes around saying "I want to be a dean when I grow up!" But I have always been invested in pedagogy, and I have a deep interest in fostering the next generation, both those who are students and those who are young faculty.

SARAH WHITING

I like to think school is about playing with all the tools in the toolbox, gaining skills to be able to approach what one might be asked to do in an office.

NEIL DENARI

It is important to teach people how to make things. It's not difficult if you have the right tools. Making things gives people hope.

KEIJI ASHIZAWA

IF YOU ARE GOING TO CONSTRUCT AN ACTUAL BUILDING THERE ARE NECESSARILY ECONOMIC FACTORS INVOLVED, BUT YOU WON'T FIND ANYBODY AT UNIVERSITY TEACHING ABOUT HOW TO DEAL WITH MONEY EVEN THOUGH IT'S SUCH AN OBVIOUS PART OF THE PROCESS.

TOYO ITO

TEACHING HELPS ME STAY SELF-CRITICAL. I AM NOT INTERESTED IN CLONING MYSELF, BUT RATHER IN GETTING STUDENTS TO THINK.

NATHALIE DE VRIES

I THINK IT HAS BEEN CLEAR FOR A LONG TIME THAT WE NEED RADICAL CHANGE AT ALL LEVELS: WHO GETS TO STUDY ARCHITECTURE, WHO GETS TO TEACH IT, AND WHO GETS TO PRACTICE IT.

MÓNICA PONCE DE LEÓN

I start my class on the first day of school and tell my students, "Allow me to tell you that I am here because I want to learn. I come to learn, that's why I teach."

TATIANA BILBAO

Teaching is also learning; teachers are in constant dialogue with themselves. I enjoyed engaging with the students, of course, but for me, the job was about my growth as much as theirs.

RICARDO SCOFIDIO

I SEE TEACHING AS A FORM OF DESIGN ADVOCACY.

BRIGITTE SHIM

I need to teach. I need a few hours in the week to talk to others about architecture.

BEN VAN BERKEL

I OFTEN TALK TO MY STUDENTS ABOUT INSECURITY. NOWADAYS THE ONLY THING THAT IS PURSUE IN SCHOOLS IS CONFIDENCE. SURELY IT IS SOMETHING TO AIM TO, BUT ONE SHOULD BE ABLE TO TOLERATE INSECURITY NEXT TO IT.

JUHANI PALLASMAA

I always had that immense belief in giving people as much control, power, responsibility as possible and let them find their breaking point. I love being a guide in that way.

THOM MAYNE

The best satisfaction comes when you discover that your student has discovered who they are, what they want to do, and that they achieve that.

ODILE DECQ

My teaching has always the same goal. To show the students a single intense moment of creative freedom. I want them to remember that once, during this studio, they were able to express themselves totally, both individually and as a group.

KARIM NADER

On reflection, African and diasporan students are the best students I have ever taught. Their capacity for imagination, creativity, and critical self-reflection is second-to-none.

LESLEY LOKKO

I want the double question of climate change and the global condition to have a radical impact on how we teach, what we teach, and how we design across the disciplines.

AMALE ANDRAOS

This younger generation really gives me hope. My students come to me and say: "I don't want to use any concrete." I say: "Wonderful! So, what do you want to use?" These values they are trying to uphold are so important.

MARINA TABASSUM

I draw and build and teach my apprentices and send them out into the world, not to be like me but to be themselves. At last count, a hundred and sixty-eight practicing architects had been trained by me at Taliesin.

FRANK LLOYD WRIGHT

I am able to teach my students what timber feels like, about its grain, tree age, density, smell—its characteristics. I couldn't effectively communicate that if I hadn't spent ten years building. I learned how to put buildings together by building them.

PETER STUTCHBURY

OUR JOB
IS NO LONGER
JUST TO TEACH.
WE SHOULD
TREAT
THESE STUDENTS
MORE LIKE
COLLABORATORS
AND PURSUE
EDUCATION
TOGETHER.

HITOSHI ABE

TIME

TIME IS IMPORTANT. THIS IS SLOW ARCHITECTURE.

KAZUYO SEJIMA

WHAT YOU NEWSPAPER AND MAGAZINE WRITERS, WHO WORK IN RABBIT TIME, DON'T UNDERSTAND IS THAT THE PRACTICE OF ARCHITECTURE HAS TO BE MEASURED IN ELEPHANT TIME.

EERO SAARINEN

IT'S NOT ONLY ABOUT BEAUTY, BUT IT'S ALSO ABOUT HOW A BUILDING PERFORMS OVER TIME. . . . THE STORY YOU'RE TELLING AT THE BEGINNING, PEOPLE WON'T KNOW OR CARE IN A HUNDRED YEARS. WHAT THEY FEEL IS THE PHYSICAL SPACE.

MA YANSONG

The most important thing for an architect today is to have time. Time to think, to change, to make models, do sketches, go to the construction site on a Saturday morning when nobody is there, take pictures. . . .

EDUARDO SOUTO DE MOURA

Although I work very hard, I don´t even see what I do as working, because I do what I love. And when that´s true, you don´t see the passage of time. You´re completely gripped, immersed in a flow.

DANIEL LIBESKIND

IT'S NOT JUST A NINE-TO-FIVE PROFESSION, IT'S 24/7. IT'S A CONSTANT PROCESS. IT'S ALMOST LIKE A LIFESTYLE.

MARINA TABASSUM

EVERY BUILDING IS A PROJECTION IN TIME.

NÍALL MCLAUGHLIN

ARCHITECTURE IS EXPOSED TO LIFE. IF ITS BODY IS SENSITIVE ENOUGH, IT CAN ASSUME A QUALITY THAT BEARS WITNESS TO THE REALITY OF PAST LIFE.

PETER ZUMTHOR

TIME IS MANAGED BY THE SUN.

ANUPAMA KUNDOO

ARCHITECT INDEX

SOURCES

ADVICE

8 "THERE IS NO AMOUNT"
Interview by Julia Gamolina, "Forms of Care: Tatiana Bilbao on Responsibility, Opportunity, and Staying True to Your 'alues," Madame Architect, December 13, 021, https://www.madamearchitect.org/nterviews/2021/11/29/tatiana-bilbao.

9 "I THINK 'JOY'"
73: Brooklyn, New York," in Louis I. Kahn: itings, Lectures, Interviews, ed. Alessandra Latour (Rizzoli, 1991), 330; originally ublished in Perspecta (Yale Architecture), no. 19 (1982): 89–100.

9 "ALWAYS HAVE A VISION"
"Architecture and the Future," IROHA, ovember 16, 2022, https://theiroha.com/blogs/architecture/hitoshi-abe.

10 "YOUR BODY IS"
terview by Salo Levinas, "Question of the nth 2—Women in Architecture," Shinberg. evinas in collaboration with LA.IDEA|DC, .d., https://www.shinberglevinas.com/news/question-of-the-month-2.

10 "YOU HAVE TO BE"
Interview by Thibaut Wychowanok, Numéro, December 22, 2015, https://umero.com/en/art-design/architecture-en/best-of-2015-interview-of-renzo-piano-the-grand-architect/.

11 "LADIES AND GENTLEMEN"
Quoted in Peter Black, Marcel Breuer: chitect and Designer (Architectural Record; Museum of Modern Art, 1949), 14.

11 "GO IN PERSON"
io Ponti, In Praise of Architecture, trans. iuseppina Salvadori and Mario Salvadori (F. W. Dodge, 1960), 134.

12 "NEVER DEMOLISH"
Celine Nguyen, "'Never Demolish. Always Transform, with and for the Inhabitants': Anne Lacaton Delivers Inaugural Jaqueline Tyrwhitt Urban esign Lecture," Harvard Graduate School of Design, April 13, 2022, https://www.gsd.harvard.edu/2022/04/never-demolish-always-transform-with-and-r-the-inhabitants-anne-lacaton-on-urban-design-and-architecture/.

12 "YOU SHOULD NOT BUILD"
Interview by Michael Bullock, "Green over Gray," PIN-UP, no. 35 (Fall/Winter 2023/24), https://www.pinupmagazine.org/articles/emilio-ambasz-interview.

13 "THERE'S ONLY ONE THING"
nterview by Alain Elkann, Alain Elkann Interviews podcast, July 28, 2024, ttps://www.alainelkanninterviews.com/amanda-levete/.

14 "GET A CONTRACT"
"Q&A: Amale Andraos," Metropolis, ptember 1, 2010, https://metropolismag.com/viewpoints/qa-amale-andraos/.

14 "THE VALUE"
Interview by Julia Gamolina, "Culture and Identity: Oshinowo Studio's Tosin Oshinowo on Calculated Risks, Apprenticeship, and Moving Forward," Madame Architect, January 31, 2024, https://www.madamearchitect.org/interviews/2024/1/16/tosin-oshinowo.

14 "THE ADVICE"
Interview by Maria Spassov, "Michael Graves on Discovering Architecture, the Rewards of Practice, and the Most Important Element of Design," ArchDaily, July 2, 2015, https://www.archdaily.com/769558/michael-graves-on-discovering-architecture-the-rewards-of-practice-and-the-most-important-element-of-design.

14 "WITHOUT OBSESSION"
Interview by Mikael Zikos, Villas, January 20, 2022, https://www.villasdecoration.com/en/design/patricia-urquiola/.

14 "WORK WITH PEOPLE"
Interview by Alexandra Khomenko, "Snarkitecture as an Open Practice," Union, n.d., https://unionmagazine.com/snarkitecture-as-an-open-practice.

14 "KEEP AT IT"
Interview by Trent Fredrickson, designboom, October 17, 2014, https://www.designboom.com/architecture/workac-interview-dan-wood-amale-andraos-10-17-2014/.

15 "NEVER LET OTHERS"
Interview by Elizabeth Sulis Gear, Something Curated, July 7, 2016, https://somethingcurated.com/2016/07/07/interview-farshid-moussavi-architect-author-professor/.

16 "OPTIMISM IS AN IMPORTANT"
Interview by Fernanda Canales, Bomb, June 16, 2025, https://bombmagazine.org/articles/2025/06/16/gabriela-carrillo-by-fernanda-canales/.

17 "BE PATIENT"
Interview by Andrea Chin, designboom, July 14, 2015, https://www.designboom.com/design/neri-hu-interview-lyndon-neri-rossana-hu-07-14-2015/.

17 "THERE'S NO TASK"
Interview by Patience Jones, As Built podcast, Graphic Machine, October 1, 2025, https://www.graphicmachine.com/podcast/marion-weiss-michael-manfredi-interview.

18 "YOU DO BETTER WORK"
Interview by Byron Kinnaird; comp. and ed. Susie Ashworth, "In Conversation with . . . Flora Samuel," Parlour, November 2, 2018, https://parlour.org.au/series/in-conversation/in-conversation-with-flora-samuel/.

18 "SELECT A PARTNER"
Interview by Richard Waite, "Alexandra Hagen of White: 'In Our Practice We Value Professional Skill over Gender,'" Architects' Journal, February 27, 2018, https://www.architectsjournal.co.uk/news/alexandra-hagen-of-white-in-our-practice-we-value-professional-skill-over-gender.

18 "HAVING THE STAMINA"
"Interview: Academic and Novelist Prof Lesley Lokko OBE," The Wick, April 29, 2024, https://thewickculture.com/interview-academic-and-novelist-lesley-lokko/.

19 "TRUST THE INVISIBLE"
Daniel Libeskind, Breaking Ground: Adventures in Life and Architecture (Riverhead Books, 2004), 208.

20 "THE ONLY REAL ADVICE"
Interview by Amir Kripper, "Top Architect: 'When I Was First Hired at Harvard, My Male Counterpart Was Paid 30% More,'" Fast Company, April 6, 2022, https://www.fastcompany.com/90737575/at-harvard-my-male-counterpart-was-paid-30-more-than-me.

20 "DON'T EVER TURN DOWN"
Victoria Kastner, Julia Morgan: An Intimate Biography of the Trailblazing Architect (Chronicle Books, 2022), 116.

21 "IF YOU HAVE ANY"
Interview by Vladimir Belogolovsky, "If You Have Any Idealism You Must Express It," STIR, October 17, 2019, https://www.stirworld.com/think-columns-if-you-have-any-idealism-you-must-express-it-says-steven-holl.

22 "DON'T YOU EVER"
Walter Gropius, "The Tree of Life Versus the Sales Spiral," in Apollo in the Democracy: The Cultural Obligation of the Architect (McGraw-Hill, 1968), 36.

22 "THERE IS AN INFINITE"
Interview by Julia Gamolina, "Imagining Worlds: Counterspace's Sumayya Vally on Optimism, Courage, and the Architecture Waiting to Be Made," Madame Architect, March 6, 2024, https://www.madamearchitect.org/interviews/2024/3/5/sumayya-vally.

22 "SELF-BELIEF IS"
Interview by Justine Clark; comp. and ed. Susie Ashworth, "In Conversation with . . . Alison Brooks," Parlour, November 21, 2019, https://parlour.org.au/series/in-conversation/in-conversation-with-alison-brooks/.

23 "BELIEVE IN GOOD"
Interview by Michael Smith, "Coincidences and Curiosity: Q+A with John Wardle and Stefan Mee," Architecture & Design, April 13, 2017, https://www.architectureanddesign.com.au/editorial/features/coincidences-and-curiosity-q-a-with-john-wardle-an.

23 "BEGIN TODAY!"
John Cairney, The Quest for Charles Rennie Mackintosh (Luath Press, 2004), 122.

ARCHITECT

24 "AN ARCHITECT'S DUTY"
Edwin Heathcote, "Minimalist Master Tadao Ando on Museum Design, Legacy, and Hope," Art Newspaper, June 23, 2023, https://www.theartnewspaper.com/2023/06/23/tadao-ando-museum-design-interview.

25 "ARCHITECTS HAVE BEEN"
Interview by Eva Prinz, Index Magazine (February/March 2005), https://www.indexmagazine.com/interviews-greg-lynn.

25 "WE HAVE THE OPPORTUNITY"
Sydney Franklin, "Becoming BIG by Starting Small: How Bjarke Ingels Worked His Way to the Top," Syracuse University School of Architecture, April 10, 2015, https://soa.syr.edu/live/news/55-becoming-big-by-starting-small-how-bjarke-ingels.

26 "YOU'VE GOT TO"
John Lloyd Wright, My Father, Frank Lloyd Wright (G. P. Putnam's Sons, 1946), 68.

27 "I DON'T BELIEVE"
James Parkes, "'Our Work Is Important, Not Us' Says RIBA International Prize Winner Kashef Chowdhury," Dezeen, April 5, 2022, https://www.dezeen.com/2022/04/05/kashef-chowdhury-riba-international-prize-winner-architecture-interviews/.

27 "THAT PERIOD"
Interview by Thom Bettridge, "Throwing Stones in Glass Boxes with Architects Liz Diller and Ellen van Loon," Interview, February 26, 2019, https://www.interviewmagazine.com/culture/throwing-stones-in-glass-boxes-with-super-architects-liz-diller-and-ellen-van-loon.

27 "I THINK THE ROLE"
Interview by Alison Cleary and Susie Ashworth; comp. and ed. Susie Ashworth, "In Conversation with . . . Yasmeen Lari," Parlour, August 31, 2018, https://parlour.org.au/series/in-conversation/in-conversation-with-yasmeen-lari/.

28 "THE ARCHITECT'S RESPONSIBILITY"
Barbie Campbell Cole and Ruth E. Rogers, Richard Rogers + Architects (St. Martins Press, 1985), 8. Quoted in Lincoln Caplan, "An Architecture of Possibilities," New Yorker, November 7, 1988, https://www.newyorker.com/magazine/1988/11/14/an-architecture-of-possibilities.

28 "BEING AN ARCHITECT"
Interview by Kim Megson, CLADmag, no. 3 (2016), https://www.spabusiness.com/index.cfm?pagetype=features&codeID=31245.

29 "THE MOST RADICAL"
Lisa Landrum, "Varieties of Architectural Imagination," Warehouse Journal, no. 25, ed. Alena Rieger and Ally Pereira-Edwards (University of Manitoba, 2016), 71.

29 "WHAT WE MAKE"
Interview by Victoria Camblin, PIN-UP, no. 36 (Spring/Summer 2024), https://www.pinupmagazine.org/articles/anupama-kundoo-interview.

ARCHITECTURE

30 "ARCHITECTURE CANNOT SAVE"
Quoted in Alvar Aalto: Objects and Furniture Design by Architects, ed. Patricia de Muga (Ediciones Poligrafa, 2007), 16.

31 "THE MEASURE OF"
Interview by Alain Elkann, Alain Elkann Interviews podcast, July 28, 2024, https://www.alainelkanninterviews.com/amanda-levete/.

31 "ARCHITECTURE ITSELF HAS"
Interview by Donald Bates, "Alison Brooks Talks Architecture's 'Role in Making People Feel Valued,'" Architecture, Au, December 19, 2018, https://architectureau.com/articles/alison-brooks-talks-career-beginnings-award-winning-works-and-design-ideals/.

31 "I DESIGN BY PUTTING"
Molly Sheridan, "Tatiana Bilbao: Architecture as a Primary Form of Care," L. Michael Goldsmith Lecture, Cornell College of Architecture, Art, and Planning, April 3, 2023, https://aap.cornell.edu/news/stories/tatiana-bilbao-architecture-as-a-primary-form-of-care/.

32 "BUILDINGS"
Daniel Libeskind, Breaking Ground: Adventures in Life and Architecture (Riverhead Books, 2004), 4.

32 "AN URGE FOR COMFORT"
Adrian Carter and Marja Sarvimäki, Jørn Utzon and Transcultural Essentialism (Routledge, 2022), xiii.

33 "I BELIEVE IN"
Quoted in Emilio Ambasz, The Architecture of Luis Barragán (Museum of Modern Art, 1976), 8.

33 "THE TERM 'ACTIONABLE IDEALISM'"
Elizabeth Glazer, "Architecture and Social Change: A Conversation with Jeanne Gang," Vital City, March 28, 2023, https://www.vitalcitynyc.org/articles/jeanne-gang-interview.

33 "I AM TOTALLY"
Nick Compton, "The 'Unpredictable' Architect Behind Victoria Beckham's Flagship Store," Wired, September 22, 2016, https://www.wired.com/story/creating-unpredictable-architecture/.

34 "ARCHITECTURE CAN BE"
Robert Venturi, "Diversity, Relevance and Representation in Historicism, or Plus ça Change . . . Plus a Plea for Pattern All Over Architecture with a Postscript on My Mother's House," Architectural Record, June 1982, 114-19; reprinted in A View from the Campidoglio: Selected Essays 1953–1984, ed. Peter Arnell, Ted Bickford, and Catherine Bergart (Harper & Row, 1984), 108–19.

34 "IT'S NOT ONLY"
"Good Architecture Is a Total Work of Art," MACH, n.d., https://www.macharch.ch/en/Journal/good-architecture-is-a-total-work-of-art/.

35 "IT IS NECESSARY THAT"
Quoted in Zeuler R. M. de A. Lima, "Lina Bo Bardi and the Architecture of Everyday Culture," Places Journal, November 2013, https://placesjournal.org/article/lina-bo-bardi-and-the-architecture-of-everyday-culture/.

36 "ARCHITECTURE IS THE MASTERLY"
Le Corbusier, "Three Reminders to Architects," in Towards a New Architecture (John Rodker, 1931), 29.

36 "ARCHITECTURE IS A FUZZY"
Rem Koolhaas, Content: Triumph of Realization (Taschen, 2004), 20.

37 "MY CONCEPT OF ARCHITECTURE"
Amy Qin, "Pritzker Prize Goes to Arata Isozaki, Designer for a Postwar World," New York Times, March 5, 2019, https://www.nytimes.com/2019/03/05/arts/design/pritzker-architecture-prize-arata-isozaki.html.

37 "ARCHITECTURE IS ABOUT"
Liu Jiakun, Pritzker Prize acceptance speec[h], May 5, 2025, https://www.pritzkerprize[.]com/ceremony-videos-liu-jiakun.

38 "I THINK GREAT ARCHITECTURE"
Interview by Andrew Wade, The Architectu[ral] League of New York, December 25, 2013, https://archleague.org/article/interview-sarah-wigglesworth/.

39 "ARCHITECTURE IS HOW"
"Kazuyo Sejima: She Can Foresee the Future of Architecture." Gentlewoma[n], no. 1 (Spring/Summer 2010), reprinted at https://thegentlewoman.co.uk/library/kazuyo-sejima.

39 "ARCHITECTURE CREATES"
Interview by Katherine Guimapang, "Deans List: Pratt's Dr. Harriet Harriss on Academia's Role in Preparing Architec[ts] of the Future," Archinect, June 24, 2019, https://archinect.com/features/article/150142013/deans-list-pratt-s-dr-harriet-harriss-on-academia-s-role-in-preparing-architects-of-the-future.

40 "ARCHITECTURE HAS NOTHING"
Interview by Emanuele Quinz, DOMUS, June 25, 2020, https://www.domusweb.i[t/]en/speciali/domusfordesign/gallery/202[0/]antonio-citterio-im-not-interested-in-revolutionizing-or-surprising-but-rather-in-getting-to-the-synthesis.html.

40 "ARCHITECTURE IS THE PLAY"
Richard Rogers, Cities for a Small Planet (Faber & Faber, 1997), 67.

41 "THE POWER OF ARCHITECTURE"
Michael Kimmelman, "Alejandro Aravena, the Architect Rebuilding a Countr[y]," New York Times Style Magazine, May 23, 2016, https://www.nytimes.com/2016/05/23/t-magazine/pritzker-venice-biennale-chile-architect-alejandro-aravena.html.

41 "ARCHITECTURE IS A PROCESS"
Interview by John Hill, "Architecture Is a Process of Translation," World-Archite[cts], May 16, 2022, https://world-architects.co[m/]en/architecture-news/insight/architecture-is-a-process-of-translation

42 "NO MATTER WHERE"
Michael Snyder, "In Niger, an Architect Looking to the Country's Design Tradition[s]," T Magazine, August 10, 2020, https://ww[w.]nytimes.com/2020/08/10/t-magazine/mariam-kamara-architect-design.html.

42 "ARCHITECTURE CAN"
Interview by Simona Falvo, "Lina Ghotme[h] and the 'Archeology of the Future,'" Architecture, Au, August 21, 2025, https:[//]architectureau.com/articles/lina-ghotme[h-]and-the-archeology-of-the-future/.

43 "TO ME, ARCHITECTURE"
Interview by Vladimir Belogolovsky, "'Architecture Is a Stage': A Q&A with Anupama Kundoo," Azure, October 8, 2021, https://www.azuremagazine.com/article/architecture-is-a-stage-a-qa-with-anupama-kundoo/.

44 "ALL BUILDING IS NOT"
"Statements on Architecture," in Louis [I.] Kahn: Writings, Lectures, Interviews, ed. Alessandra Latour (Rizzoli, 1991), 22[…] from a talk given at the Politecnico diMila[no], January 1967.

44 "I LOVE ARCHITECTURE"
Interview by Nam Kiwanuka, Vhat Is Great Architecture?" TVO Today, August 4, 2023, https://www.tvo.org/transcript/2752776.

44 "THERE IS A DEFINING"
Dabbagh Architects Rethinks Traditional References in Dubai Mosque Design hrough Form and Materiality," DE51GN, December 19, 2021, https://de51gn. /dabbagh-architects-rethinks-traditional-references-in-dubai-mosque-design-through-form-and-materiality/.

45 "ARCHITECTURE MUST MOVE YOU"
rview by Massimo De Conti, "Marcio Kogan: chitecture Must Move You!"" Klat, October , 2016, https://www.klatmagazine.com/ /architecture-en/marcio-kogan/53770.

BEAUTY

46 "I THINK THE CHANCE"
Michael Kimmelman, "The Ascension of ter Zumthor," New York Times Magazine, March 11, 2011, https://www.nytimes.com/2011/03/13/magazine/mag-13zumthor-t.html.

47 "ALL OF US NEED"
"Jacques Herzog Meets Tatiana Bilbao," video conversation, Louisiana Channel, ouisiana Museum of Modern Art, Afasia chzine, May 2019, https://afasiaarchzine.com/2019/09/jacques-herzog-meets-tatiana-bilbao/.

47 "WE BELIEVE IN"
erview by Patrick Kasingsing, "The Future Is a Journey to the Past: A Conversation th Mario Cucinella," Kanto, December 20, 2023, https://kanto.ph/voices/mario-cucinella/.

48 "I THINK THAT WE"
oe Tennant, "Architect Douglas Cardinal on Building in Harmony with Nature," CBC Radio, April 1, 2021, https://www. c.ca/radio/unreserved/how-indigenous-chitects-are-resisting-colonial-legacies-l-reshaping-spaces-1.5971556/architect-uglas-cardinal-on-building-in-harmony-with-nature-1.5972742.

48 "I SPENT MY CHILDHOOD"
mily Priest, "Juhani Pallasmaa on Beauty and the Beholder," RIBAJ, July 5, 2019, https://www.ribaj.com/culture/an-interview-with-juhani-pallasmaa.

49 "BEAUTY IS AN ORACLE"
nterview by Christian Narkiewicz-Laine 981), reprinted at "Architecture of Silence: Interview with Luis Barragán," Global Design News, January 11, 2021, https://globaldesignnews.com/architecture-f-silence-interview-with-luis-barragan/.

50 "I AM NOT INTERESTED"
Interview by Vladimir Belogolovsky, "Interview with Peter Eisenman: 'I Am Not Convinced that I Have a Style,'" rchDaily, April 11, 2016, https://www. rchdaily.com/785334/interview-with-peter-eisenman-i-am-not-convinced-that-i-have-a-style.

50 "SOME ARCHITECTURE IS"
Interview by Hans Ulrich Obrist and Rem Koolhaas, in Hans Ulrich Obrist: Interviews, vol. 2, ed. Charles Arsène-Henry, Shumon Basar, and Karen Marta (Edizione Charta, 2010), 253.

50 "I LOVE THINGS"
Stefan Sagmeister, "Diller Scofidio + Renfro's Liz Diller in Conversation with Stefan Sagmeister," Wallpaper*, September 30, 2015, https://www.wallpaper.com/architecture/diller-scofidio-renfro-liz-diller-in-conversation-with-stefan-sagmeister.

51 "I LOVE THINGS"
Aldo Rossi, A Scientific Autobiography, trans. Lawrence Venuti (MIT Press; Graham Foundation for Advanced Studies in the Fine Arts; Institute for Architecture and Urban Studies, 1981), 82.

52 "BEAUTY IS THE PEAK"
Interview by Vladimir Belogolovsky, "Interview with Álvaro Siza: 'Beauty Is the Peak of Functionality!'" ArchDaily, January 11, 2017, https://www.archdaily.com/803250/interview-with-alvaro-siza-beauty-is-the-peak-of-functionality.

52 "REAL BEAUTY"
Quoted in Kenneth Frampton, "The Legacy of Alvar Aalto: Evolution and Influence," in Alvar Aalto: Between Humanism and Materialism, ed. Peter Reed (Museum of Modern Art, 1998), 119.

53 "THE PUBLIC OFTEN THINKS"
Brian Bethune, "Why Moshe Safdie Wants Canada to Rebuild Its Sense of Adventure," Macleans, August 24, 2022, https://macleans.ca/the-interview/why-moshe-safdie-wants-canada-to-rebuild-its-sense-of-adventure/.

53 "IT'S IMPORTANT TO ME"
Interview by Magali Robathan, CLADMag, no. 1 (2020), https://www.cladglobal.com/architecture-design-features?codeid=34348&source=home&p=10.

54 "TAKE NOTHING FOR GRANTED"
"To the Young Man in Architecture," in Frank Lloyd Wright: Writings and Buildings, comp. and ed. Edgar Kaufmann and Ben Raeburn (Meridian, 1960), 250; originally published in Two Lectures in Architecture (Art Institute of Chicago, 1931).

54 "BEAUTY WILL RESULT FROM"
Andrea Palladio, The Four Books of Architecture, Book 1 (R. Ware, 1738), 1.

55 "FOR ME, BEAUTY IS SYNONYMOUS"
"'Architecture Is a Tool to Improve Lives': Interview with Anna Heringer," UnternehmerTUM, February 9, 2022, https://www.unternehmertum.de/en/topics/sustainability/architektur-improves-lives-interview-anna-heringer.

CHILDHOOD

56 "I'VE ALWAYS WANTED"
Interview by Ugonna-Ora Owoh, Interior Design, March 14, 2023, https://interiordesign.net/designwire/10-questions-with-tosin-oshinowo/.

57 "WHEN I WAS FIVE"
Interview by Falen Johnson, "How Growing Up in Foster Care Shaped Nisga'a Architect Patrick Stewart's Work," CBC Radio, April 1, 2021, https://www.cbc.ca/radio/unreserved/how-indigenous-architects-are-resisting-colonial-legacies-and-reshaping-spaces-1.5971556/how-growing-up-in-foster-care-shaped-nisga-a-architect-patrick-stewart-s-work-1.5971645.

57 "I WAS VERY MUCH"
Interview by Eliza Scarborough, "A&E Interviews: Antonia Citterio and Patricia Viel Unveil a New Jewel to Bulgari's Crown," Adam & Eve (a&e), January 16, 2018, https://aeworld.com/lifestyle/luxury-living-italian-design-duo-antonio-citterio-and-patricia-viel-unveil-a-new-jewel-to-bvlgaris-crown/.

58 "OUR PARLOR CEILING"
Richard Neutra, Survival Through Design (Oxford University Press,1954), 25.

58 "SOMETIMES I CAN"
Peter Zumthor, "A Way of Looking at Things," in Thinking Architecture (Birkhäuser, 1999), 9.

59 "WHEN I WAS ABOUT NINE"
Conversation Between Camilla Block and Qianyi Lim, "The Age We're In," Powerhouse Museum, n.d., https://powerhouse.com.au/stories/camilla-block-x-qianyi-lim.

60 "ONE OF MY EARLIEST"
"Yvonne Farrell and Shelley McNamara Biography," The Pritzker Architecture Prize, n.d., https://www.pritzkerprize.com/laureates/2020#laureate-page-2161.

60 "MY GRANDMOTHER"
"Frank Gehry Started Off Building Cities with His Grandma," More with Anna Maria Tremonti, CBC podcast, March 10, 2020, https://www.cbc.ca/radio/podcastnews/frank-gehry-started-off-building-cities-with-his-grandma-1.5491434.

61 "WHEN I WAS VERY LITTLE"
Jonathan Glancey, "'I Pick Up My Pen. A Building Appears,'" The Guardian, August 1, 2007, https://www.theguardian.com/artanddesign/2007/aug/01/architecture.

62 "MY MOTHER'S FRIENDS"
Interview by Aileen Kwun and Bryn Smith, Twenty Over Eighty: Conversations on a Lifetime in Architecture and Design (Princeton Architectural Press, 2016), 53.

62 "SOME VIVID MEMORIES"
Interview by Julia Gamolina, "Over and Over: Hilary Sample on Making Books, Crafting an Office, and Leading a Creative Life," Madame Architect, May 6, 2020, https://www.madamearchitect.org/interviews/2020/5/4/hilary-sample.

62 "I WAS OBSESSED"
Interview by Johnny Tucker, "'I Got Here by Sticking to My Guns': Nicholas Grimshaw on Winning the RIBA Royal Gold Medal," FX Design, February 14, 2019, https://www.fxdesign.co.uk/legibility-adaptability-et-sustainability-6988570/?cf-view.

62 "WHEN I WAS A CHILD"
"Interview: Sumaya Dabbagh on Work, Identity, and Gender," Architect, April 15, 2018, https://www.middleeastarchitect.com/insight/interview-sumaya-dabbagh-on-work-identity-and-gender.

62 "WHEN I WAS TWELVE"
Interview by Carson Chan, "Greg Lynn: Curve Your Enthusiasm," 032c, no. 15 (Summer 2008), https://web.archive.org/web/20100628082247/http://032c.com/2008/greg-lynn-curve-your-enthusiasm/.

63 “WHEN I WAS ELEVEN OR TWELVE”
Interview by Guy Horton, “Inside the Mind of Sou Fujimoto,” Metropolis, November 14, 2018, https://metropolismag.com/profiles/inside-the-mind-of-sou-fujimoto/?utm_medium=website&utm_source=archdaily.com.

63 “I LEFT SCHOOL”
Introduction to Le Corbusier: The Complete Works 1910–1929, vol. 1, ed. Willy Boesiger and Oscar Stonorov (Birkhäuser, 1995), 13.

64 “WHILE I WAS GROWING UP”
“Rahul Mehrotra of RMA Architects,” Modelo, n.d., https://modelo.io/blog/index.php/rahul-mehrotra-of-rma-architects/.

64 “I REMEMBER THE ROOM”
“Francis Kéré Biography,” The Pritzker Architecture Prize, n.d., https://www.pritzkerprize.com/laureates/diebedo-francis-kere#laureate-page-2421.

64 “BACK THEN”
Christoph Elhardt, “Overcoming Modernism’s Blinkered View,” My Science, October 8, 2024, https://www.myscience.org/news/wire/overcoming_modernism_s_blinkered_view-2024-ethz.

64 “WHEN I WAS A KID”
Interview by Elsbeth Ronner, “Point Supreme Architects Bringing Back Greekness,” Archined, April 14, 2017, https://www.archined.nl/2017/04/point-supreme-architects/.

64 “I WAS FOURTEEN”
Interview by Catherine Hong, “How Deborah Berke Became One of Architecture’s Most Visible Women,” Surface, December 10, 2019, https://www.surfacemag.com/articles/deborah-berke-architect/#.

65 “WHEN OTHER BOYS”
Interview by Stephen Heyman, “Striking a Balance,” T Magazine blog, April 9, 2014, https://archive.nytimes.com/tmagazine.blogs.nytimes.com/2014/04/09/architecture-striking-a-balance/.

66 “BY SECOND OR THIRD GRADE”
Louis Menand, “Maya Lin, the Reluctant Memorialist,” New Yorker, July 1, 2002, https://www.newyorker.com/magazine/2002/07/08/maya-lin-the-reluctant-memorialist.

66 “ONE DAY”
Louis Kahn, “Structure Is a Design in Light: The Notebooks of Louis I. Kahn,” Paris Review, February 8, 2022, https://www.theparisreview.org/blog/2022/02/08/structure-is-a-design-in-light-the-notebooks-of-louis-i-kahn/.

67 “I LOOK AT PICTURES”
Interview by Derek Blasberg, “In Conversation: Annabelle Selldorf,” Gagosian Quarterly, March 17, 2015, https://gagosian.com/quarterly/2015/03/17/annabelle-selldorf/.

67 “YOU KNOW”
John Seabrook, “The Abstractionist,” New Yorker, December 13, 2009, https://www.newyorker.com/magazine/2009/12/21/the-abstractionist.

CLIENTS

68 “THERE IS NO GOOD”
“Souto de Moura and Pallasmaa in Dialogue,” Arquitectura Viva, October 30, 2017, https://arquitecturaviva.com/articles/souto-de-moura-and-pallasmaa-in-dialogue.

69 “I WOULD NEVER”
Interview by Alyn Griffith, “‘I’d Love to Design a Brothel or a Gas Station’ Says Brazilian Architect Isay Weinfeld,” Dezeen, November 18, 2013, https://www.dezeen.com/2013/11/18/isay-weinfeld-interview/.

69 “OF COURSE WE DO NOT”
Interview by Andrew Mackenzie, “Rem Koolhaas: National Identity in Architecture,” Architecture, Au, March 25, 2014, https://architectureau.com/articles/national-identity-in-architecture-an-interview-with-rem-koolhaas/.

70 “I NEED TO TRULY”
Interview by Natalie Stoclet, “The Human Side of Art and Architecture with Vincent Van Duysen,” Forbes, June 21, 2023, https://www.forbes.com/sites/nataliestoclet/2023/06/21/the-human-side-of-art-and-architecture-with-vincent-van-duysen/.

70 “RATHER THAN ‘EDUCATING’”
Interview by Evelina Pa, “Keiji Ashizawa on Honest Design and the Interplay of Space, Interiors, and Objects,” Branding in Asia, August 26, 2025, https://www.brandinginasia.com/keiji-ashizawa-on-honest-design-and-the-interplay-of-space-interiors-and-objects/.

70 “PEOPLE HAVE ALWAYS”
Ana Bogdan, “Francine Houben: ‘What’s Most Important Is the Senses,’” The Talks, n.d., https://the-talks.com/interview/francine-houben/.

71 “RESIDENTS NEED”
“Architecture / Q&A,” Icon, February 2017, https://www.lacatonvassal.com/data/documents/20181213-1205571702_ICON.pdf.

72 “NEVER TALK TO A CLIENT”
“Conversation One” (1959), in Conversations with Mies van der Rohe (Princeton Architectural Press, 2008), 17.

72 “ONE OF THE SECRETS”
Interview by Michael Bullock, PIN-UP, no. 35 (Fall/Winter 2023/24), https://www.pinupmagazine.org/articles/emilio-ambasz-interview.

73 “THIS IS REALLY”
Interview by Joana Lazarova, “Architecture Is the Testimony of the Time It Is Set In. . . ,” Scale, July 28, 2020, https://scalemag.online/architecture/architecture-is-the-testimony-of-the-time-it-is-set-in/.

73 “QUITE A LOT OF PEOPLE”
Interview by Thom Bettridge, “Throwing Stones in Glass Boxes with Architects Liz Diller and Ellen van Loon,” Interview, February 26, 2019, https://www.interviewmagazine.com/culture/throwing-stones-in-glass-boxes-with-super-architects-liz-diller-and-ellen-van-loon.

73 “CLIENTS!”
Interview by Aileen Kwun and Bryn Smith, Twenty Over Eighty: Conversations on a Lifetime in Architecture and Design (Princeton Architectural Press, 2016), 167.

74 “I HAVE ALWAYS BEEN”
Quoted in Michael Eaude, Critical Lives: Antoni Gaudí (Reaktion Books, 2024), 89.

74 “YOU CANNOT MAKE”
Interview by Danny Hudson, designboom, April 15, 2013, https://www.designboom.com/architecture/shelley-mcnamara-of-grafton-architects-interview/.

75 “I STARTED WORKING”
Interview by Alain Elkann, Alain Elkann Interviews podcast, October 1, 2023, https://www.alainelkanninterviews.com/peter-marino-3/.

76 “I TRY TO MAINTAIN”
Interview by Rachel Pulfer, “Shigeru Ban: Temporary Architecture Is Made to Last,” Azure, March 2, 2020, https://www.azuremagazine.com/article/shigeru-ban-interview/.

76 “I OFTEN TELL”
“Yasmeen Lari: ‘On the Road to Self-Reliance,’” Al Jazeera, August 12, 2014, https://www.aljazeera.com/video/rebe architecture/2014/8/12/yasmeen-lari-on-the-road-to-self-reliance.

77 “I DON’T THINK”
Interview by Judy Hudson, Bomb, April 2001, https://bombmagazine.org/articles/2001/04/01/samuel-mockbee

COLLABORATION

78 “ARCHITECTURE IS TOO IMPORTANT”
Ian Parker, “Norman Foster’s Empire of Image Control,” New Yorker, January 2 2025, https://www.newyorker.com/magazine/2025/01/27/norman-foster-pr

79 “THERE IS NO IMMACULATE”
Quoted in Paul Keskeys, “Listen to Thes Words of Wisdom from Denise Scott Brown, the ‘Grandmother of Architecture Architizer, n.d., https://architizer.com/blog/practice/materials/denise-scott-bro the-grandmother-of-architecture/.

79 “I THINK THE COLLECTIVE”
Interview by Kevin Crouse and Giacomo Sartorelli, “On Writing: Kunlé Adeyemi, Modern Usage, Spring 2017, reprinted at https://volume-1.org/2017-2018-O Writing-Kunle-Adeyemi.

80 “I STILL HAVE A PENCIL”
Interview by Alain Elkann, Alain Elkann Interviews podcast, January 26, 2020, https://www.alainelkanninterviews.com/renzo-piano-2/.

80 “OUR DESIGN PROCESS”
Interview by Y-Jean Mun-Delsalle, “Davi Rockwell Celebrates the 30th Anniversa of His Architecture and Design Firm,” Forb December 26, 2014, https://www.forbe com/sites/yjeanmundelsalle/2014/12/26/david-rockwell-celebrates-the-30 anniversary-of-his-architecture-and-design-firm/.

80 “IT’S A VERY FLAT”
Interview by Kriston Capps, “Studio Vis with La Dallman,” Architect Magazine, June 6, 2012, https://www.architectmagaz com/design/firm-profile/studio-visit-wi la-dallman_o.

81 “THINKING COLLECTIVELY”
Interview by Bodil Blain, “Out of Office: Co and Creative Small Talk with Kjetil Træd Thorsen,” Wallpaper*, October 12, 202 https://www.wallpaper.com/design/kje traedal-thorsen-snohetta-interview.

81 “I DON’T HAVE”
Interview by Alison Beard, “Life’s Work An Interview with Daniel Libeskind,” Harv Business Review, July–August 2018, https hbr.org/2018/07/lifes-work-an-intervie with-daniel-libeskind.

82 "THE 'COMMITTEE MEETING'"
tegorical Reply to Questions by 'Architecture of the U.S.S.R,'" in Frank Lloyd Wright llected Writings, ed. Bruce Brooks Pfeiffer (Rizzoli, 1993), 145.

82 "I WOULD PREFER"
nversation One" (1959), in Conversations with Mies van der Rohe (Princeton Architectural Press, 2008), 24.

83 "HOW DO THREE PEOPLE"
Interview by Junko Kawakami, Houzz, ay 29, 2017, https://www.houzz.com.sg/ gazine/a-chat-with-pritzker-prize-2017- eates-rcr-architects-stsetivw-vs~86605333.

83 "WE HAVE TO STOP"
Interview by Andrea Chin, designboom, pril 8, 2016, https://www.designboom. com/architecture/antonio-citterio- patricia-viel-interview-04-08-2016/.

83 "WE HAVE A RULE"
Speech to the attendees at the Women Architecture Luncheon, March 2, 2018, printed at https://www.architectsjournal. .uk/news/amanda-levete-theres-never- been-a-better-time-to-be-a-woman-we- have-to-seize-this-moment.

84 "UNDERSTAND THE IMPORTANCE"
'International Women's Day: A Postcard My Younger Self," BBC Arts, March 8, 2016, ttps://www.bbc.co.uk/programmes/art cles/2khp5zWQ9Wmv0Y33bgpT8dk/ rnational-womens-day-a-postcard-to-my- younger-self.

84 "COMPETITION IS NOT"
Interview by Marcus Trimble, rchitecture, Au, May 14, 2012, https:// itectureau.com/articles/glenn-murcutt/.

84 "IN THE PAST"
nterview by Susie Ashworth and Justine Clark; comp. and ed. Susie Ashworth, Conversation with . . . Jude Barber," Parlour, July 11, 2020, https://parlour.org.au/ eries/in-conversation/in-conversation- with-jude-barber/.

85 "ARCHITECTURE IS THE ART"
'Lina Ghotmeh Is Reimagining Cultural itecture for a Connected World," Observer, December 29, 2025, https://observer. om/2025/12/interview-lina-ghotmeh- useums-architecture-global-dialogue/.

COMMUNITY

86 "DIALOGUE IS"
rview by Thomas Roueché, TANK Magazine, o. 102 (Spring 2025), https://tank.tv/ azine/issue-102/talks/alvaro-siza-vieira.

87 "THERE IS NO HOUSE"
nterview by John Hill, "No House Exists Isolation," video conversation, Louisiana annel, Louisiana Museum of Modern Art, orld-Architects, June 20, 2025, https:// w.world-architects.com/en/architecture- ews/film/no-house-exists-in-isolation.

87 "IT TAKES A VILLAGE"
Tosin Oshinowo (@tosin.oshinowo), stagram, August 7, 2022, https://www. instagram.com/p/Cg9LEmIjUiN/.

88 "YOU HAVE TO BRING"
e People's Architect, Conscious Company agazine, July/August 2016, 84, https:// ch.co.uk/wp-content/uploads/2017/03/ 2016-SW-Conscious-Co-Mag__profile.pdf.

88 "WHEN WE CAN"
Interview by Andrea-Jo Wilson, "Q&A: Brian Porter, Principal, Two Row Architect," Foyer, June 28, 2023, https://readfoyer.com/article/ qa-brian-porter-principal-two-row-architect.

89 "I ALWAYS"
Amanda Short, "Meet Three Architects and Educators Who Are Engaging Indigenous Communities to Help Them Facilitate Their Own Visions for the Future," Indigenous Land Urban Stories, n.d., https://indigenouslandurbanstories.ca/ portfolio-item/building-solutions/.

89 "I AM MOST PROUD"
Interview by Shumi Bose, PIN–UP, no. 28 (Spring/Summer 2020), https://archive. pinupmagazine.org/articles/interview-2020- architect-francis-kere.

CONFESSIONS

90 "WHAT I REALLY"
Interview by Vladimir Belogolovsky, "'What I Really Like Is Speed': In Conversation with Odile Decq," ArchDaily, January 8, 2020, https://www.archdaily.com/931493/ what-i-really-like-is-speed-in-conversation- with-odile-decq.

91 "PYRAMIDS"
Gio Ponti, In Praise of Architecture, trans. Giuseppina Salvadori and Mario Salvadori (F. W. Dodge, 1960), 63.

91 "I DO NOT LIKE"
"Not for the Fainthearted," in Louis I. Kahn: Writings, Lectures, Interviews, ed. Alessandra Latour (Rizzoli, 1991), 262; originally published in AIA Journal 55, no. 6 (June 1971).

91 "WHEN I STARTED"
"Souto de Moura and Pallasmaa in Dialogue," Arquitectura Viva, October 30, 2017, https:// arquitecturaviva.com/articles/souto-de- moura-and-pallasmaa-in-dialogue.

92 "I DO READ"
Interview by Veronica Simpson, FX Design, May 19, 2014, https://www.fxdesign.co.uk/ frank-gehry-4271271/.

92 "THE FEMALE PHILOSOPHER"
Interview by Kasumiko Murakami; trans. Hikari Hida, Mastermind, n.d., https:// mastermindparis.com/features/a- conversation-with-riken-yamamoto-pritzker- prize-winning-architect/.

92 "PEOPLE SAY"
Interview by Robert Locke, "Peter Eisenman: 'Liberal Views Have Never Built Anything of Any Value,'" Archinect, July 27, 2004, https:// archinect.com/features/article/4618/peter- eisenman-liberal-views-have-never-built- anything-of-any-value.

93 "SOME YEARS AGO"
Interview by Begoña Marín Calle, Cosentino, n.d., https://www.cosentino.com/blog/ interview-with-alberto-campo-baeza/.

93 "I'M NOT OBSESSIVE"
Interview by Craig Kellogg, "10 Questions with . . . Deborah Berke," Interior Design, August 1, 2017, https://interiordesign.net/ designwire/10-questions-with-deborah-berke/.

94 "WHEN I WAS A CHILD"
Interview by Leeji Choi, designboom, October 29, 2005, https://www.designboom. com/interviews/sanaa-kazuyo-sejima-ryue- nishizawa-designboom-interview/.

94 "MANY YEARS AGO"
Interview by Rem Koolhaas, "New Again: Zaha Hadid," Interview, February 2005, reprinted athttps://www.interviewmagazine. com/art/new-again-zaha-hadid.

94 "TO THIS DAY"
"The Nature of Materials," in Frank Lloyd Wright: Writings and Buildings, comp. and ed. Edgar Kaufmann and Ben Raeburn (Meridian, 1960), 223; originally published in Architectural Record (1928).

94 "I LOVE WHEN"
Interview by Vladimir Belogolovsky, "Wolf Prix: Gravity? No, Thank You!" Curatorial Project, November 2008, http://curatorialproject.com/interviews/ wolfprix.html.

94 "SECRETLY, I'VE ALWAYS"
Interview by Justine Clark; comp. and ed. Susie Ashworth, "In Conversation with . . . Julie Eizenberg," Parlour, September 17, 2019, https://parlour.org.au/series/ in-conversation/in-conversation-with- julie-eizenberg/.

94 "MY FAVORITE OBJECT"
Interview by Jan Henderson, Australian Design Review, April 22, 2016, https:// www.australiandesignreview.com/interiors/ pushing-boundaries-with-manuelle-gautrand/.

94 "I OFTEN DREAM"
Interview by Sukie Smith, "Charlotte Skene Catling: A Rebel with a Cause," Lab Mag, 100.

94 "I WANT TO DIE"
Interview by Alison Beard, "Life's Work: An Interview with Renzo Piano," Harvard Business Review, https://hbr. org/2025/09/lifes-work-an-interview- with-renzo-piano.

95 "I WOULD RATHER"
Ellen C. Soroka, "Visit to Carlo Scarpa's Studio (Sept. 11, 1978)," in "Carlo Scarpa: Connections in Design: A Generic Attitude" (master's thesis, Massachusetts Institute of Technology, 1973), 102, https://dspace.mit. edu/handle/1721.1/29840.

CREATIVE PROCESS

96 "WHEN I START"
Interview by Michael Bullock, "Jeanne Gang: A Midwestern Architect Who Is Taking the World by Storm," PIN–UP, no. 13 (Fall/Winter 2012/13), https://archive. pinupmagazine.org/articles/architect- jeanne-gang-interview.

97 "THE START"
Snarkitecture (Phaidon, 2018), 236.

97 "WHEN I'M WORKING"
Daniel Libeskind, Breaking Ground: Adventures in Life and Architecture (Riverhead Books, 2004), 127.

97 "I ALWAYS RESEARCH"
Interview by Bill Moyers, "A Conversation with Maya Lin," Moyers, April 25, 2003, https://billmoyers.com/content/ maya-lin-extended/.

98 "I TAKE LOTS OF NOTES"
Interview by Diana Budds, "21 Questions: Liz Diller Wears Zippered Sweatpants to Black-Tie Events," Curbed (New York Magazine), April 14, 2023, https://www.curbed.com/2023/04/ architect-liz-diller-interview-21-questions.html.

98 "FIRST I GATHER"
Interview by Alain Elkann, Alain Elkann Interviews podcast, January 12, 2020, https://www.alainelkanninterviews.com/jean-nouvel/.

98 "WHEN THE PROJECTS"
"Subversion, Silence, and Normality," interview in Renzo Piano and Building Workshop: Buildings and Projects 1971–1989 (Rizzoli, 1989), 237.

99 "NEARLY EVERY DESIGN"
Juhani Pallasmaa, "Aalto: Toward a Synthetic Functionalism," in Alvar Aalto: Between Humanism and Materialism (Museum of Modern Art, 1998), 21.

99 "I'M REMINDED"
Interview by Valeria Molinari, Teatro dell'architettura Mendrisio, April 2, 2020, https://www.tam.usi.ch/en/feeds/30407.

100 "WHAT'S EXCITING"
"Architect Spotlight: Camilla Block," Brickworks, February 26, 2021, https://www.brickworks.com.au/articles/architect-spotlight-camilla-block/.

100 "IN EACH PROJECT"
"Pre-theoretical Ground," in The Steven Holl Catalogue (Artemis and Arc en rêve centre d'architecture, 1993), 21.

101 "HERE IN THE OFFICE"
Interview by Vladimir Belogolovsky, " 'Architecture Is Like Writing a Song': In Conversation with Rick Joy," ArchDaily, April 13, 2021, https://www.archdaily.com/959818/architecture-is-like-writing-a-song-in-conversation-with-rick-joy.

DOWNTIME

102 "I GO SWIMMING"
Interview by Begoña Marín Calle, Cosentino, n.d., https://www.cosentino.com/blog/interview-with-alberto-campo-baeza/.

103 "I LISTEN"
Interview by Andrea Canclini, Aya Jazaierly, Miloš Ćipranić, Petar Bojanić, Pierre-Alain Croset, and Snežana Vesnić, "The Right to Beauty: Interview with Álvaro Siza," Khōrein 3, no. 1 (2025), https://khorein.ifdt.bg.ac.rs/index.php/ch/article/view/82/69.

103 "MY GRANDMOTHER"
Nic Monisse, "Richard England's Architectural World in Malta," Monocle, no. 177 (September 2, 2024), https://monocle.com/design/a-piece-of-england-in-malta/.

104 "WEDNESDAY IS MY DAY"
Interview by Romullo Baratto, "Gloria Cabral: 'Everything Begins with the Wisdom of a Place,'" trans. Diogo Simões, ArchDaily, January 24, 2024, https://www.archdaily.com/1012261/gloria-cabral-everything-begins-with-the-wisdom-of-a-place.

104 "I LOVE FLOATING"
Interview by Alain Elkann, Alain Elkann Interviews podcast, January 26, 2020, https://www.alainelkanninterviews.com/renzo-piano-2/.

104 "I'M AN EXTREME SKIER"
"Interview with Architect Cazú Zegers," Vibia, n.d., https://vibia.com/us/interview-with-architecht-cazu-zegers/.

104 "FLIGHT FOR ME"
Interview by Christopher Turner, Icon, August 9, 2011, https://www.iconeye.com/architecture/interview-norman-foster.

104 "I LOVE TO COOK"
Interview by Julia Gamolina, "Forms of Care: Tatiana Bilbao on Responsibility, Opportunity, and Staying True to Your Values," Madame Architect, December 13, 2021, https://www.madamearchitect.org/interviews/2021/11/29/tatiana-bilbao.

105 "I WOULDN'T SAY"
Interview by Eliza Scarborough, "A&E Interviews: Antonia Citterio and Patricia Viel Unveil a New Jewel to Bulgari's Crown," Adam & Eve (a&e), January 16, 2018, https://aeworld.com/lifestyle/luxury-living-italian-design-duo-antonio-citterio-and-patricia-viel-unveil-a-new-jewel-to-bvlgaris-crown/.

DRAWING

106 "I DRAW"
Interview by Alain Elkann, Alain Elkann Interviews podcast, January 12, 2020, https://www.alainelkanninterviews.com/jean-nouvel/.

107 "THE CREATOR"
"Instead of an Article," Arkkitehti-Arkitekten (1958), reprinted at https://drawingmatter.org/aalto-instead-of-an-article/.

107 "THE PLEASURE"
Interview by Myrto Katsikopoulou, "Inside MK27's Cinematic Architecture: Marcio Kogan Discusses New Rizzoli Monograph," designboom, May 29, 2024, https://www.designboom.com/architecture/marcio-kogan-mk27-cinematic-monograph-rizzoli-interview-05-29-2024/.

108 "I THINK WE ALL"
"On the Responsibility of the Architect," in Louis I. Kahn: Writings, Lectures, Interviews, ed. Alessandra Latour (Rizzoli, 1991), 53; originally published in Perspecta (Yale Architecture), no. 2 (1953): 47–50.

108 "EVERY MEETING"
Graduation speech, University of Technology Sydney, 2014, reprinted at https://www.uts.edu.au/for-students/current-students/managing-your-course/graduation/speakers-and-speeches/2014/ms-camilla-block.

109 "MOST OF THE DRAWINGS"
Fredi Fischli and Niels Olsen, "Stones, Inflatables, and Ephemera: The Chilean Architect's Fragile Vision of Architecture," PIN–UP, no. 37 (Fall/Winter 2024/25), https://www.pinupmagazine.org/articles/smiljan-radic-interview.

109 "MY SKETCHES"
William Hanley, "Sketchbook: Liz Diller," Surface, March 27, 2017, https://www.surfacemag.com/articles/architecture-sketchbook-liz-diller/.

110 "DRAWINGS SERVE"
Interview by Karen Wong, "A New Project from Annabelle Selldorf, the Art World's Favorite Architect, Plays Against Type," Cultured, March 19, 2024, https://www.culturedmag.com/article/2024/03/19/annabelle-selldorf-architect-new-york/.

111 "THE VERB"
Interview by Andrea Oppenheimer Dean "Interview with 2009 AIA Gold Medal Winner Glenn Murcutt," Architectural Record, May 16, 2007, https://www.architecturalrecord.com/articles/6029-interview-with-2009-aia-gold-medal-winner-glenn-murcutt.

111 "I DON'T USE"
Interview by Philip Stevens, "Interviews with Zaha Hadid: The Architect's Work in Her Own Words," designboom, March 31, 2016, https://www.designboom.com architecture/zaha-hadid-interview-quote dies-aged-65-03-31-2016/.

112 "MY STAFF HAS TO BE ABLE"
Interview by Anne Rieselbach, "In Conversation: Marlon Blackwell and Rick Joy," The Architectural League, n.d., https://archleague.org/article/in-conversation-marlon-blackwell-and-rick-joy/.

112 "WE BEGIN"
Jonathan Glancey, "Sanaa's Summer Pavili Brings Sunshine to the Serpentine," The Guardian, July 8, 2009, https://www theguardian.com/artanddesign/2009/jul/08/sanaa-summer-pavilion-serpentir

112 "IT'S A COMPLEX THING"
Quoted in Andrew Ayers, "Book Club: The Strange Drawn Worlds of Claude Parent," PIN-UP, n.d., https:/ archive.pinupmagazine.org/articles/book-club-claude-parent-drawing-rizzol andrew-ayers.

113 "FOR ME"
Akiva Blander, "On Indigenous Peoples' D Revisiting the Meaning of 'Native Architectu Metropolis, October 14, 2019, https:// metropolismag.com/viewpoints/studio indigenous-chris-cornelius/.

114 "THE SKETCH"
Interview by Andrea Canclini, Aya Jazaier Miloš Ćipranić, Petar Bojanić, Pierre-Ala Croset, and Snežana Vesnić, "The Right t Beauty: Interview with Álvaro Siza," Khōr 3, no. 1 (2025), https://khorein.ifdt.bg.ac index.php/ch/article/view/82/69.

114 "THE DRAWN LINE"
Lebbeus Woods, "Line," in Slow Manifes (Princeton Architectural Press, 2015), 2

115 "ON AN AIRPLANE"
Interview by Allison Berry, "The Creativ Mind: Q&A with Artist and Architect Ma Lin," Time, May 2, 2013, https://style.tir com/2013/05/02/the-creative-mind-q with-artist-and-architect-maya-lin/.

115 "EVERY LINE"
Interview by Alana Pockros, "Drawing Every Line for Every Consciousness: Elle van Loon," Spike, June 29, 2023, https:/ spikeartmagazine.com/articles/intervie ellen-van-loon-factory-international-20

116 "SOMETIMES"
Daniel Libeskind, Breaking Ground: Adventures in Life and Architecture (Riverhead Books, 2004), 7.

116 "WHEN I HAVE LOOKED"
Interview by Jonathan Glancey, "I Pick Up My Pen. A Building Appears," The Guardian, August 1, 2007, https:/ www.theguardian.com/artanddesign/2007/aug/01/architecture.

117 "WHEN WE DREW"
Interview by Amy Frearson, "Merging Architecture and Landscape 'Came Very Naturally' to Snøhetta Says Co-Founder," Dezeen, December 11, 2019, https://ww.dezeen.com/2019/12/11/snohetta-interview-kjetil-traedal-thorsen-30th-anniversary-architecture/.

DREAM PROJECTS

118 "I WOULD LIKE"
Interview by Alain Elkann, Alain Elkann Interviews podcast, October 11, 2020, ttps://www.alainelkanninterviews.com/emilio-ambasz/.

119 "I'VE ALWAYS"
"Tei Carpenter with Ayesha Ghosh," Brooklyn Rail, November 2024, https://rooklynrail.org/2024/11/architecture/tei-carpenter-with-ayesha-ghosh/.

119 "I WANT TO"
d Loos, "The Architect Kulapat Yantrasast Loves 'Making Good Spaces,'" New York nes, May 24, 2018, https://www.nytimes.om/2018/05/24/arts/design/kulapat-yantrasast-architect.html.

120 "I'VE ALWAYS WANTED"
nterview by Craig Kellogg, "10 Questions with... Deborah Berke," Interior Design, August 1, 2017, https://interiordesign.net/designwire/10-questions-with-deborah-berke/.

120 "I WOULD LIKE"
nterview by Magali Robathan, CLADMag, . 1 (2017), https://www.cladglobal.com/pdf/CLADmag_issue1_2017.pdf.

121 "A FOOTBALL STADIUM"
Interview by Jordi Lippe-McGraw, "Legendary Architect David Rockwell Reveals His Dream Project," Forbes, May 23, 2018, https://www.forbes.com/sites/jordilippemcgraw/2018/05/23/rchitect-david-rockwell-dream-project/.

121 "I WANT TO BUILD"
nterview by Cécilia Pelloux, "An Inspiring Conversation with Art and Architecture aestro Peter Marino," Forbes, December 2, 2019, https://www.forbes.com/sites/ciliapelloux/2019/12/02/an-inspiring-onversation-with-art-and-architecture-maestro-peter-marino/.

121 "MY DREAM PROJECT"
Interview by Ljubov Dzuzhynska, Aught, n.d., https://aughtmag.com/articles/slava-balbek.

122 "I DREAM OF THE DAY"
nterview by Caitlin St. John, "4 Women chitects and Designers Tell Their Stories," Hospitality Design, March 31, 2021, https://hospitalitydesign.com/people/terviews/women-architects-designers/.

122 "THE IDEA OF BUILDING"
nterview by Oliva Sartogo, "Bjarke Ingels: Architecture as an Evolving Process," alone del Mobile.Milano, April 6, 2025, printed at https://www.salonemilano.it/en/articles/bjarke-ingels-interview.

123 "I'VE NEVER DONE"
nterview by Aaron Britt, "Interview with Jürgen Mayer H.: Part II," Dwell, February 12, 2009, https://www.dwell.com/article/interview-with-jurgen-mayer-h.-part-ii-56b17b5e.

123 "I READ AN INTERVIEW"
Interview by Derek Blasberg, "In Conversation: Annabelle Selldorf," Gagosian Quarterly, March 17, 2015, https://gagosian.com/quarterly/2015/03/17/annabelle-selldorf/.

124 "I WOULD LIKE"
Interview by Jan Dominik Geipel, "Origin and Attitude," Detail Architecture, December 4, 2023, https://www.detail.de/de_en/herkunft-und-haltung?srsltid=AfmBOoq4zKt6UA0a1yp19g29Fpnf36M68hz_fs1EmFH9rtbHM6tLkc3r.

125 "I REMAIN OPEN"
Interview by Ulf Meyer, "Building a Modest Utopia," World-Architects, March 23, 2022, https://www.world-architects.com/en/architecture-news/insight/building-a-modest-utopia.

125 "I AM TOO SUPERSTITIOUS"
"5 Questions for Frank Gehry," Hospitality Design, November 2, 2015, https://hospitalitydesign.com/people/interviews/5-questions-for-frank-gehry/.

FASHION

126 "JUMPSUITS ALWAYS"
Interview by Karen Wong, "Architect Kulapat Yantrasast Is Bringing His Boundless Imagination to the Met's Arts of Africa, Ancient America, and Oceania Galleries," Cultured, November 21, 2024, https://www.culturedmag.com/article/2024/11/21/architect-kulapat-yantrasast-met-museum-interview/.

127 "LEATHER IS MY THING"
Interview by Malaika Byng, Wallpaper*, April 27, 2010, https://www.wallpaper.com/art/peter-marino-interview.

127 "I WEAR ONLY BLACK"
Interview by Diana Budds, "21 Questions: Liz Diller Wears Zippered Sweatpants to Black-Tie Events," Curbed (New York Magazine), April 14, 2023, https://www.curbed.com/2023/04/architect-liz-diller-interview-21-questions.html.

128 "I DON'T SPEND"
Interview by Richelle [Sibolboro], designboom, November 19, 2012, https://www.designboom.com/architecture/greglynn-interview/.

128 "I LIKE LOOSE"
Interview by Danny Hudson, designboom, April 15, 2013, https://www.designboom.com/architecture/shelley-mcnamara-of-grafton-architects-interview/.

128 "THE LAST THING"
Interview by Christina Ohly Evans, "The Aesthete: Jean Nouvel Talks Personal Taste," Christina Ohly Evans, n.d., https://www.christinaohlyevans.com/blog-1/esidszpk4pu9dtapsvo3jvvp0an0om.

129 "I HAVE BEEN TRAPPED"
"Odile Decq," ArchIdea 62 Interview, Forbo, December 2020, https://www.forbo.com/flooring/en-uk/inspiration-references/making-spaces-into-places-blog/odile-decq-archidea-interview/pgmrpu.

129 "I DON'T DRESS LIKE"
Interview by Robert Locke, "Peter Eisenman: 'Liberal Views Have Never Built Anything of Any Value,'" Archinect, July 27, 2004, https://archinect.com/features/article/4618/peter-eisenman-liberal-views-have-never-built-anything-of-any-value.

FUTURE

130 "THE FUTURE PROJECTS"
Alice Rawsthorn, "Eileen Gray, Freed from Seclusion," New York Times, February 24, 2013, https://www.nytimes.com/2013/02/25/arts/design/eileen-gray-freed-from-seclusion.html.

131 "I AM LOOKING"
Interview by Ulf Meyer, "Building a Modest Utopia," World-Architects, March 23, 2022, https://www.world-architects.com/en/architecture-news/insight/building-a-modest-utopia.

131 "I AM INCREDIBLY BAD"
Paul Fraioli, "Reinventing the City: An Interview with Architect Rem Koolhaas," Christian Science Monitor, July 20, 2012, https://www.csmonitor.com/Commentary/Global-Viewpoint/2012/0720/Reinventing-the-city-An-interview-with-architect-Rem-Koolhaas.

132 "WE ONLY CREATE"
Interview by Susan Piedmont-Palladino, National Building Museum, October 31, 2006, https://nbm.org/lessons-in-arcology-an-interview-with-paolo-soleri/.

132 "THE FUTURE IS A JOURNEY"
Interview by Patrick Kasingsing, "The Future Is a Journey to the Past: A Conversation with Mario Cucinella," Kanto, December 20, 2023, https://kanto.ph/voices/mario-cucinella/.

132 "THE FUTURE IS A SPREADING"
Interview by Guy Horton, "'The Future Is a Spreading Matrix': In Conversation with Sou Fujimoto," ArchDaily, November 21, 2018, https://www.archdaily.com/906059/the-future-is-a-spreading-matrix-in-conversation-with-sou-fujimoto.

133 "THINGS WE CANNOT"
Introduction to Le Corbusier: The Complete Works 1910–1929, vol. 1, ed. Willy Boesiger and Oscar Stonorov (Birkhäuser, 1995), 13.

133 "EVENTUALLY"
Interview by Jane Szita, "Winy Maas on the Green Dip," Iconic Houses, March 22, 2021, https://www.iconichouses.org/news/ihc20-winy-maas-on-the-green-dip.

134 "MY LIFE AMBITION"
Interview by Lori Ferriss, "'My Life's Ambition Is to Become Redundant': Yasmeen Lari, Pakistan's First Female Architect, on Decarbonization and Decolonization," Architizer, n.d., https://architizer.com/blog/inspiration/stories/yasmeen-lari-decarbonization-decolonization/.

135 "THE ARCHITECTS"
Interview by Katie Watkins, ArchDaily, December 3, 2014, https://www.archdaily.com/573785/ad-interviews-kunle-adeyemi-nle.

135 "FOR SO LONG"
Interview by Kate Nelson, "Sam Olbekson Is Decolonizing Design, One Building at a Time," Architectural Digest, November 24, 2022, https://www.architecturaldigest.com/story/sam-olbekson-decolonizing-design-interview.

136 "DESIGNING FOR LONGEVITY"
Nic Monisse, "How Architect Jeanne Gang Is Reshaping Cities Through Purposeful Design," Monocle, May 20, 2025, https://monocle.com/design/jeanne-gang-interview/.

136 "I PERSONALLY WANT"
Interview by Emma Robertson, "Tadao Ando: 'There Is No Such Thing as Creation from Nothing,'" The Talks, n.d., https://the-talks.com/interview/tadao-ando/.

137 "WE ARE IN A WORLD"
Interview by Rowan Moore, "Farshid Moussavi: 'We Are in a World Where Ideas Migrate,'" The Guardian, November 15, 2014, https://www.theguardian.com/artanddesign/2014/nov/16/farshid-moussavi-interview-victoria-beckham-mayfair-store-rowan-moore.

138 "TODAY IS THE FIRST DAY"
Interview by Nic Monisse, "Norman Foster on What Good Design Really Means When Reinventing Cities," Monocle, July 1, 2025, https://monocle.com/design/norman-foster-interview-venice-biennale/.

138 "WE ARE ALWAYS"
Interview by Andrea Chin, designboom, April 8, 2016, https://www.designboom.com/architecture/antonio-citterio-patricia-viel-interview-04-08-2016/.

139 "THE FUTURE IS OUR"
Quoted in Arthur Thompson, "Sérgio Bernardes," Icon, January 19, 2015, https://www.iconeye.com/opinion/sergio-bernardes.

GENDER

140 "I WAS ALWAYS"
Quoted in Mary Anne Hunting and Kevin D. Murphy, Women Architects at Work (Princeton University Press, 2025), 4.

141 "IF YOU GOOGLE"
Interview by Nam Kiwanuka, TVO Today, August 4, 2023, https://www.tvo.org/transcript/2752776.

141 "I DIDN'T WANT"
Amy Waldman, "Jeanne Gang in the Wild," New Yorker, May 12, 2014, https://www.newyorker.com/magazine/2014/05/19/the-urban-wild.

142 "BY 1900"
Lois Lilley Howe, "An Alumna's Architectural Career," Technology Review, 66, no. 2 (December 1963), 21, 38. Quoted in Women Architects at Work (Princeton University Press, 2025), 9.

143 "THE PROFESSION IS NOT"
Interview by Jon Astbury, Architects' Journal, February 7, 2018, https://www.architectsjournal.co.uk/news/stephanie-macdonald-of-6a-i-am-so-impressed-by-the-generations-of-women-coming-after-me.

143 "RARELY ARE WOMEN"
Dorte Mandrup, "I Am Not a Female Architect. I Am an Architect," Dezeen, May 25, 2017, https://www.dezeen.com/2017/05/25/dorte-mandrup-opinion-column-gender-women-architecture-female-architect/.

144 "THE PRIMARY LESSON"
Interview by Lan Anh Vu, "How I Got There: Caroline Bos," Huffington Post, October 7, 2015, https://www.huffpost.com/entry/how-i-got-there-caroline_b_8247344.

144 "AT MY AGE"
Interview by Julia Gamolina, "A Broader Vision: MVRDV's Nathalie de Vries on Running a Business, Reinventing Practice, and Leading by Example," Madame Architect, March 4, 2020, https://www.madamearchitect.org/interviews/2020/3/3/nathalie-de-vries.

144 "WE NEED TO CELEBRATE"
Interview by Susie Ashworth and Justine Clark; comp. and ed. Susie Ashworth, "In Conversation with . . . Madhavi Desai," Parlour, July 18, 2020, https://parlour.org.au/series/in-conversation/in-conversation-with-madhavi-desai/.

145 "I'VE NEVER HEARD"
Interview by Simon Hattenstone, "Master Builder," The Guardian, February 3, 2003, https://www.theguardian.com/artanddesign/2003/feb/03/architecture.artsfeatures.

146 "I WAS RECENTLY"
Interview by Christina Ohly Evans, "Deborah Berke's Clean and Simple Spaces," Christina Ohly Evans, n.d., https://www.christinaohlyevans.com/blog-1/qkb6qmp3wbm6kz4cvssuzgtyau5t6n.

146 "I AM LOOKING FORWARD TO"
"Interview with Manuelle Gautrand, Women Architect of the Year," Aesthetica, June 24, 2015, https://aestheticamagazine.com/interview-with-manuelle-gautrand-women-architect-of-the-year/.

147 "IT'S VERY INTERESTING"
Interview by Jan Dominik Geipel, "Social Commitment," Detail, December 11, 2023, https://www.detail.de/de_en/soziales-engagement.

148 "I WAS TOLD"
Interview by Edwin Heathcote, "Architect Itsuko Hasegawa: 'I Was Told Girls Don't Go to Technical Universities,'" Financial Times, July 13, 2018, https://www.ft.com/content/ce04c3e4-8367-11e8-a29d-73e3d454535d.

148 "I SOMETIMES GO"
Nell Card, "No House of Straw: Sarah Wigglesworth's Eco-Home, 20 Years On," The Guardian, June 7, 2020, https://www.theguardian.com/artanddesign/2020/jun/07/return-sarah-wigglesworth-straw-bale-house-stock-orchard-street.

149 "FIFTY PERCENT"
Interview by Laura Traldi, "I'm Still 'Against' but from the Inside," DesignAtLarge, April 18, 2019, https://www.designatlarge.it/elizabeth-diller-interview/?lang=en

150 "WHEN I STARTED"
Interview by Marie Davidová, Collaborative Collective, Archiweb, April 25, 2018, https://www.archiweb.cz/en/n/interview/interview-with-odile-decq.

150 "IT TOOK A LONG TIME"
Interview by Justine Clark; comp. and ed. Susie Ashworth, "In Conversation with . . . Alison Brooks," Parlour, November 21, 2019, https://parlour.org.au/series/in-conversation/in-conversation-with-alison-brooks/.

151 "KNOW THE BARRIERS"
Interview by Justine Clark; comp. and ed. Susie Ashworth, "In Conversation with . . . Julie Eizenberg," Parlour, September 17, 2019, https://parlour.org.au/series/in-conversation/in-conversation-with-julie-eizenberg/.

HOUSE + HOME

152 "MY HOUSE IS MY REFUGE"
Emilio Ambasz, The Architecture of Luis Barragán (Museum of Modern Art, 1976), 8.

153 "IF THE HOUSE"
Frank Lloyd Wright to Miss Rose Pauson, August 4, 1939, Letters to Clients, ed. Bruce Brooks Pfeiffer (Architectural Press, 1987), 192.

153 "THE HOUSE IS A HOME"
Quoted in Derya Yorgancioğlu, "Steven Ho[…] A Translation of Phenomenological Philoso[…] into the Realm of Architecture" (master's thesis, Middle East Technical University, 20[…] https://doi.org/10.7761/978973199737[…]

153 "EACH OF OUR PROJECTS"
"The Green Blueprint," Prestige Magazine, July 13, 2024, https://theprestige.global/the-green-blueprint/.

154 "I LIKE THE SPACE"
Interview by Alejandra González Romo, "How the Architect Frida Escobedo Think[…] About Art and Design," trans. Enrique Pér[…] Rosiles, Aperture, no. 238 (Spring 2020), reprinted at https://aperture.org/editoria[…] how-the-architect-frida-escobedo-thinks-about-art-and-design/.

154 "I TRY TO DESIGN HOMES"
Margherita Guccione, "Cini Boeri: Designi[…] Is a Joy, but Also a Commitment," Domus, May 9, 2012, https://www.domusweb.it/en/interviews/2012/05/09/cini-boeri-designing-is-a-joy-but-also-a-commitment.html.

155 "THE HOUSE IS A MACHINE"
Le Corbusier, "Argument," in Towards a New Architecture (John Rodker, 1931), 4[…]

156 "FOR ME THE IDEA"
Níall McLaughlin, "Architects' Homes," Níall McLaughlin Architects, n.d., https://www.niallmclaughlin.com/mediafiles/filer_public/56/66/56660319-c15a-4ea[…]8b61-298e5d2bebe6/homes.pdf.

157 "THE HOME IS LIKE"
Interview by Mathures Paul, "Architect Anupama Kundoo on Her Creation—Wal[…] House, Which Is Now Being Celebrated on Apple TV+ Series Home," Telegraph (Indi[…] April 19, 2020, https://www.telegraphind[…]com/entertainment/architect-anupama-kundoo-on-her-creation-wall-house-which-now-being-celebrated-on-the-apple-tv-ser[…]home/cid/1766260#goog_rewarded.

157 "AT MY HOUSE"
"The Village Collection by Salvatori: An Interview with Vincent Van Duysen," Salvatori, March 2022, https://www.salvatoriofficial.com/en-us/us/stories/th[…]village-collection-interview-vincent-van-duysen/.

158 "I HAVE THIS DREAM"
"Beyond the Blueprint: An In-Depth Joh[…] Pawson Interview," Gessato, n.d., https://www.gessato.com/beyond-blueprint-john-pawson/.

158 "A HOUSE IS"
Interview by Katherine Adomaitis, "Keeping Up with the Joneses," Phoenix Home + Garden, September 3, 2019, https://www.phgmag.com/keeping-up-with-the-joneses/.

159 "HOME IS WHERE"
Interview by Nicole Ex, "The Homemak[…] and His Doman: Bijoy Jain and His Mumb[…] Home," See All This, no. 32 (December 20[…] https://seeallthis.com/en/interview/bij[…]jain-the-homemaker-and-his-domain/

HUMILITY

160 "AMBIGUITY IS A WELCOME"
Selldorf Architects: Portfolio and Projects (Phaidon, 2016), afterword.

161 "DON'T BE AFRAID"
Graduation speech, University of chnology Sydney, 2014, https://www.uts.edu.au/for-students/current-students/anaging-your-course/graduation/speakers-and-speeches/2014/ms-camilla-block.

161 "I STILL FEEL"
Interview by Tom Ravenscroft, "'I Don't Believe I'm That Talented,' Says Pritzker Winner David Chipperfield," Dezeen's ce to Face podcast, March 7, 2023, https://www.dezeen.com/2023/03/07/david-chipperfield-interview-pritzker-winner/.

162 "I FEEL LIKE"
Interview by Oliver Wainwright, The Barefoot Architect: 'I Was a Starchitect 36 Years. Now I'm Atoning,'" The Guardian, ril 1, 2020, https://www.theguardian.com/tanddesign/2020/apr/01/yasmeen-lari-pakistan-architect-first-female-jane-drew.

162 "I HAVE NEVER CONSIDERED"
Interview by Josh Harris, "Architecture Is Choreography: In Conversation with uhani Pallasmaa," Architecture, Au, n.d., https://architectureau.com/articles/itecture-is-choreography-in-conversation-with-juhani-pallasmaa/.

162 "GO FOR ANY PROJECT"
Interview by Pratyush Sarup, In an Exclusive Interview, Norman Foster peaks on AI, Modern Cities, and the Power of Good Design," Architectural Digest, October 12, 2025, https://www.architecturaldigest.com/story/norman-foster-life-lessons-from-the-worlds-greatest-architect.

163 "WE MUST TRY"
Jonathan Glancey, "'I Pick Up My Pen. A Building Appears,'" The Guardian, ugust 1, 2007, https://www.theguardian.n/artanddesign/2007/aug/01/architecture.

164 "TO BE A GOOD ARCHITECT"
Interview by Ingerid Helsing Almaas, "People Have to Be Strong to Cope with Good Architecture," Arkitektur N, May 10, 2010, https://www.architecturenorway.no/stories/people-stories/fehn-97/.

164 "GONE ARE THE DAYS"
nterview by Nour Fakharany, "Redefining African Architecture Through Context Collaboration," ArchDaily, November 27, 2024, https://www.archdaily.com/1024037/tosin-oshinowo-redefining-african-architecture-through-context-and-collaboration.

164 "I LIKE THE TEACHINGS"
terview by Whitney Mallett, "Indigenous Architect Douglas Cardinal on Care, ommunity, and His Architecture's Sense Spirit," PIN–UP, no. 32 (Spring/Summer 022), https://www.pinupmagazine.org/articles/douglas-cardinal-interview.

164 "THERE IS NO LONGER"
rriet Harriss, "Five Ways that Architecture Education Needs to Change," Dezeen, ovember 27, 2025, https://www.dezeen.m/2025/11/27/architecture-education-harriet-harriss-performance-review/.

164 "YOU KNOW"
Interview by Vladimir Belogolovsky, "Glenn Murcutt: 'Any Work of Architecture That Exists or Has a Potential to Exist Is There to Be Discovered,'" Curatorial Project, September 2013, http://curatorialproject.com/interviews/glennmurcutt.html.

165 "DARE TO BE"
Buckminster Fuller, Synergetics: Explorations in the Geometry of Thinking (Macmillan, 1975), xix.

IDENTITY

166 "I HAVE FOUGHT"
Louis Menand, "Maya Lin, the Reluctant Memorialist," New Yorker, July 1, 2002, https://www.newyorker.com/magazine/2002/07/08/maya-lin-the-reluctant-memorialist.

167 "WHEN I LOOK"
Interview by Vladimir Belogolovsky, "Interview with Peter Eisenman: 'I Am Not Convinced That I Have a Style,'" ArchDaily, April 11, 2016, https://www.archdaily.com/785334/interview-with-peter-eisenman-i-am-not-convinced-that-i-have-a-style.

167 "I'VE ALWAYS BEEN"
John Seabrook, "The Abstractionist," New Yorker, December 13, 2009, https://www.newyorker.com/magazine/2009/12/21/the-abstractionist.

167 "I NEVER THOUGHT"
Zoe Tennant, "Architect Douglas Cardinal on Building in Harmony with Nature," CBC Radio, April 1, 2021, https://www.cbc.ca/radio/unreserved/how-indigenous-architects-are-resisting-colonial-legacies-and-reshaping-spaces-1.5971556/architect-douglas-cardinal-on-building-in-harmony-with-nature-1.5972742.

168 "I SEE MYSELF"
Interview by Jan Dominik Geipel, "Origin and Attitude," Detail Architecture, December 4, 2023, https://www.detail.de/de_en/herkunft-und-haltung.

168 "I APPRECIATE"
Interview by Oluwatobiloba Ajayi, Dada, no. 2, https://freight.cargo.site/m/U22385342386430799541515558694895/_DADA-ISSUE-2---MASTER-DOC-FINAL-FILE_yusuff.pdf.

168 "MANY ARCHITECTS USE"
"Pritzker Prize Goes to . . . Liu Jiakun of China, An Architect Who Celebrates Lives of Ordinary Citizens," Macau Daily Times, December 29, 2025, https://macaudailytimes.com.mo/liu-jiakun-of-china-an-architect-who-celebrates-lives-of-ordinary-citizens.html/.

169 "I FEEL THAT CHINA"
Quoted in Jiayang Fan, "I. M. Pei and the Asian-American Experience," New Yorker, May 17, 2019, https://www.newyorker.com/news/daily-comment/i-m-pei-and-the-asian-american-experience.

170 "I'M A WANDERER"
Interview by Nicole Ex, "The Homemaker and His Domain: Bijoy Jain and His Mumbai Home," See All This, no. 32 (December 2023), https://seeallthis.com/en/interview/bijoy-jain-the-homemaker-and-his-domain/.

171 "IF THERE IS"
Walter Gropius, "The Inner Compass," in Apollo in the Democracy: The Cultural Obligation of the Architect (McGraw-Hill, 1968), 15.

171 "I HAVE SEVEN"
Brendan Gill, "Outside the Profession," New Yorker, September 26, 1953, https://www.newyorker.com/magazine/1953/09/26/outside-the-profession.

INFLUENCE

172 "ALVAR AALTO'S WORK"
Robert Venturi, "Alvar Aalto," in A View from the Campidoglio: Selected Essays 1953–1984, ed. Peter Arnell, Ted Bickford, and Catherine Bergart (Harper & Row, 1984), 60.

173 "ONE OF MY GREAT SOURCES"
Ellen C. Soroka, "Carlo Scarpa: Connections in Design: A Generic Attitude" (master's thesis, Massachusetts Institute of Technology, 1973), 102, https://dspace.mit.edu/handle/1721.1/29840.

173 "CARLO SCARPA'S APPROACH"
Anton Giuroiu, "Interview with Di Zhang and Jack Young of waa," Architecture Lab, October 23, 2024, https://www.architecturelab.net/interview-with-di-zhang-and-jack-young-of-waa/.

173 "I WAS INFLUENCED"
Interview by Judy Hudson, Bomb, April 1, 2001, https://bombmagazine.org/articles/2001/04/01/samuel-mockbee/.

174 "I ADMIRE ANTONI GAUDÍ"
Interview by Niall Patrick Walsh, "'I Seek to Create an Escape from Everyday Life'; A Conversation with Ma Yansong of MAD Architects," Archinect, October 15, 2022, https://archinect.com/features/article/150326692/i-seek-to-create-an-escape-from-everyday-life-a-conversation-with-ma-yansong-of-mad-architects.

174 "I WAS ALWAYS INTRIGUED"
Interview by Stephen Todd, "In Conversation with . . . Shigeru Ban," Habitus, n.d., https://www.habitusliving.com/articles/in-conversation-with-shigeru-ban.

175 "WHATEVER I HAVE LEARNED"
Lazar D. Kesic, "Rafiq Azam: The Poetry of Architecture and Watercolors of Bangladesh," AIA New York, August 14, 2014, https://www.aiany.org/news/rafiq-azam-the-poetry-of-architecture-and-watercolors-of-bangladesh/.

176 "I DID LIKE"
Interview by Suleman Anaya, "Agustín Hernández's Futuristic Monoliths Inspired by Mesoamerican Architecture," PIN–UP, n.d., https://archive.pinupmagazine.org/articles/interview-agustin-hernandez-sci-architecture-mexico-suleman-anaya.

176 "EARLY ON"
Interview by Luis Fernández-Galiano, Arquitectura Viva, January 7, 2021, https://arquitecturaviva.com/articles/jacques-herzog-al-final-emprendimos-un-viaje-propio.

177 "THE WORK"
Aldo Rossi, A Scientific Autobiography (MIT Press; Graham Foundation for Advanced Studies in the Fine Arts; Institute for Architecture and Urban Studies, 1981), 37.

177 "IT'S A BIT OF A CLICHÉ"
Interview by Christina Pazzanese, The Harvard Gazette, May 16, 2018, https://news.harvard.edu/gazette/story/2018/05/architect-toshiko-mori-on-her-work-teaching-and-path-to-harvard/.

177 "I THINK WE ARE ALL"
Interview by Gerrit Terstiege, Rams Foundation, n.d., https://rams-foundation.org/magazine/interviews/foster/.

178 "I THINK LE CORBUSIER"
Interview by Andrea Chin, designboom, April 8, 2016, https://www.designboom.com/architecture/antonio-citterio-patricia-viel-interview-04-08-2016/.

178 "LE CORBUSIER"
Eero Saarinen, "Dickinson College Arts Award Address," in Shaping the Future (Yale University Press ; Finnish Cultural Institute; Museum of Finnish Architecture; The National Building Museum; Yale University School of Architecture, 2006), 347.

178 "AUGUSTE PERRET"
Introduction to Le Corbusier: The Complete Works 1910–1929, vol. 1, ed. Willy Boesiger and Oscar Stonorov (Birkhäuser, 1995), 11.

179 "LE CORBUSIER"
Interview by Leeji Choi, designboom, October 29, 2005, https://www.designboom.com/interviews/sanaa-kazuyo-sejima-ryue-nishizawa-designboom-interview/.

180 "THE PERSON I ALWAYS"
Interview by Michael Bullock, "Jeanne Gang: A Midwestern Architect Who Is Taking the World by Storm," PIN–UP, no. 13 (Fall/Winter 2012/13), https://archive.pinupmagazine.org/articles/architect-jeanne-gang-interview.

180 "THE NEW YORK GUGGENHEIM"
Interview by Delphine Roche, Numéro, September 9, 2020.

181 "ONE OF MY STRONGEST"
Tadao Ando: Conversations with Students, trans. and ed. Matthew Hunter (Princeton Architectural Press, 2012), 59.

182 "AT ARCHITECTURE SCHOOL"
Interview by Begoña Marín Calle, Cosentino, n.d., https://www.cosentino.com/blog/interview-with-alberto-campo-baeza/.

183 "THE ARCHITECTURE OF NIEMEYER"
Interview by Romullo Baratto, "'It's Not Because You Are Limited in Resources that You Should Accept Mediocrity,'" ArchDaily, September 24, 2021, updated March 15, 2022, https://www.archdaily.com/968831/its-not-because-you-are-limited-in-resources-that-you-should-accept-mediocrity-interview-with-francis-kere.

183 "I WANT TO BE LIKE"
Interview by Massimo De Conti, "Marcio Kogan 'Architecture Must Move You!'" Klat, October 27, 2016, https://www.klatmagazine.com/en/architecture-en/marcio-kogan/53770.

INSPIRATION

184 "A SUNSET"
Interview by Emmanuel Olunkwa, "Washing Clay," PIN–UP, no. 35 (Fall/Winter 2023/24), https://www.pinupmagazine.org/articles/sumayya-vally-interview.

185 "FOR ME"
Interview by Andy Butler, designboom, August 12, 2013, https://www.designboom.com/architecture/frida-escobedo-interview/000.

185 "WHEN I WAS EIGHTEEN"
Interview by Vladimir Belogolovsky, "Wolf Prix: Gravity? No, Thank You!" Curatorial Project, November 2008, http://curatorialproject.com/interviews/wolfprix.html.

186 "I STILL REMEMBER"
Interview by Delphine Roche, Numéro, September 9, 2020.

186 "I AM ALWAYS IN AWE"
"Q&A with Jeanne Gang," Te Kāhui Whaihanga New Zealand Institute of Architects, February 2024.

187 "I AM MUCH MORE INSPIRED"
Interview by Alyn Griffith, "'I'd Love to Design a Brothel or a Gas Station' Says Brazilian Architect Isay Weinfeld," Dezeen, November 18, 2013, https://www.dezeen.com/2013/11/18/isay-weinfeld-interview/.

188 "OFTEN WHEN OUR SON"
Ingerid Helsing Almaas, "Peripheral Vision: An Interview with Tod Williams and Billie Tsien," Arkitektur N, June 6, 2013, https://www.architecturenorway.no/stories/people-stories/williamstsien-13/.

188 "WHEN I WAS A TEENAGER"
Interview by Valeria Molinari, Teatro dell'architettura Mendrisio, April 2, 2020, https://www.tam.usi.ch/en/feeds/30407.

188 "WHEN BEGINNING"
Interview by Josh Harris, "Architecture Is Choreography: In Conversation with Juhani Pallasmaa," Architecture, Au, n.d., https://architectureau.com/articles/architecture-is-choreography-in-conversation-with-juhani-pallasmaa/.

189 "I HAVE RECENTLY"
"Carla Juaçaba: 'For Me, Material and Context Are Intrinsically Related,'" Architectural Record, May 27, 2015, https://www.architectural-review.com/essays/profiles-and-interviews/carla-juacaba-for-me-material-and-context-are-intrinsically-related.

189 "WHEN I LOOK"
Interview by Reiji Yamakura, "Interview with Keiji Ashizawa / Keiji Ashizawa Design—part 2," trans. Richard Streeby, Idreit, n.d., https://idreit.com/en/article/2020/2/interview-with-keiji-ashizawa-keiji-ashizawa-design-part-2.

190 "I LIKE MONUMENTAL"
Interview by Ljubov Dzuzhynska, Aught, n.d., https://aughtmag.com/articles/slava-balbek.

191 "I HAVE UNDENIABLY"
Interview by Suleman Anaya, "Agustín Hernández's Futuristic Monoliths Inspired by Mesoamerican Architecture," PIN–UP, n.d., https://archive.pinupmagazine.org/articles/interview-agustin-hernandez-sci-architecture-mexico-suleman-anaya.

191 "THE LESSONS LEARNED"
Interview by Christian Narkiewicz-Laine (1981), reprinted at "Architecture of Silence: Interview with Luis Barragán," Global Design News, January 11, 2021, https://globaldesignnews.com/architecture-of-silence-interview-with-luis-barragan/.

192 "THERE IS NOTHING"
Interview by Caroline Brand, "Santiago Calatrava's Extraordinary Designs," B Beyond, n.d., https://www.bbeyondmagazine.com/santiago-calatrava-interview-architecture-art-legacy/.

192 "I LIKE THE IDEA"
Interview by Vladimir Belogolovsky, "'A Va[...] May Give a Shape to a Room," ArchDaily, September 29, 2020, https://www.archda[...] com/948643/a-vase-may-give-a-shape-to[...] room-in-conversation-with-john-wardle[...]

193 "I LOVE TO PEOPLE-WATCH"
Interview by Visual Collaborative, March [...] 2019, https://www.visualcollaborative.co[...] tosin_oshinowo_lagos/.

LIGHT

194 "THE SUN NEVER KNEW"
"Architecture," The John William Lawren[...] Memorial Lectures (1972), in Louis I. Kah[...] Writings, Lectures, Interviews, ed. Alessan[...] Latour (Rizzoli, 1991), 277.

195 "ONE CAN CREATE"
Interview by Mark Edward Harris, "'I Will Never Give Up Creating, Because [...] Create Is to Live,'" Vanity Fair, April 7, 2025, https://www.vanityfair.com/style[...] story/interview-with-architect-tadao-and[...] sltid=AfmBOorCcPeXZ2CNvytvdBvCo3U[...] i38bIAkbzSblezAvXhPEvJdSoc.

195 "NATURAL LIGHT"
Interview by Emma Robertson, "Kengo Kuma: 'Light Gives Us a Message,[...] The Talks, n.d., https://the-talks.com/interview/kengo-kuma/.

196 "I HAVE ALWAYS"
Ben Luke, "Frank Gehry on LUMA Arles: 'I Kept Thinking About What the Light Was Like for Van Gogh,'" Art Newspaper, June 23, 2021, https://www.theartnewspaper.com/2021/06/23/frank-gehry-on-luma-arles-i-kept-thinking-about-what-the-light-was[...] like-for-van-gogh.

196 "LIGHT DOESN'T JUST ILLUMINATE[...]
Interview by Sophie Lewis, "Where Architects Live | Joris Poggioli," est, n.d., https://estliving.com/where-architects-live-joris-poggioli/.

196 "ONE OF THE CONSTANT"
Interview by Alain Elkann, Alain Elkann[...] Interviews podcast, January 26, 2020, https://www.alainelkanninterviews.com[...] renzo-piano-2/.

197 "WE CHASE THE SUN"
Sophie Lovell, David Thulstrup: A Sens[...] of Place (Phaidon, 2023), 148.

198 "BEDROOMS AND LIBRARIES"
Vitruvius: The Ten Books on Architectur[...] trans. Morris Hicky Morgan, Book VI (Harv[...] University Press, 1914), 181.

198 "LIGHT IS THE 'CLUE' MATERIAL"
Interview by Meghna Mehta, "Dreaming[...] Reality," Mondo*arc India, no. 15 (July/August 2017), reprinted at https://www[...] stirworld. com/inspire-people-dreaming-reality.

199 "IN MY ARCHITECTURE"
"Interview: Vincent Van Duysen," est, n.d., https://estliving.com/interview-vincent-van-duysen/.

199 "WITHOUT LIGHT"
Mariann Eliassen, "No Architecture With[...] Light—Rick Joy Interview," D/A (Dayligh[...] and Architecture), June 12, 2018, https:[...] www.daylightandarchitecture.com/news/[...] architecture-without-light-rick-joy-intervi[...]

MATERIALS

200 "WORKING WITH WOOD"
terview by Emma Robertson, "Kengo Kuma: Light Gives Us a Message,"" The Talks, n.d., https://the-talks.com/interview/kengo-kuma/.

201 "ADOLF LOOS"
Interview by Alison Beard, "Life's Work: n Interview with Daniel Libeskind," Harvard usiness Review , July–August 2018, https://br.org/2018/07/lifes-work-an-interview-with-daniel-libeskind.

201 "AN ARCHITECT MUST"
Adrian Carter and Marja Sarvimäki, preface o Jørn Utzon and Transcultural Essentialism (Routledge, 2022).

201 "[TREES] HAVE A LIFE"
Interview by Marc-Christoph Wagner, "'Wood Can Connect the Simple and the ublime': In Conversation with Helen & Hard Architects," video conversation, Louisiana Channel, Louisiana Museum of Modern Art, rchDaily, February 15, 2023, https://www.archdaily.com/tag/siv-helene-stangeland.

202 "WE HAVE TO ACCEPT"
Interview by Terence Gower, Bomb, arch 18, 2015, https://bombmagazine.org/articles/2015/03/18/tatiana-bilbao/.

202 "I LOVE THE STONE"
Cathleen McGuigan, "Gehry with a French Twist," Newsweek, June 12, 1994, https://www.newsweek.com/gehry-french-twist-188946.

202 "WE STARTED WORKING"
nterview by Ilana Herzig, "Frida Escobedo on Building Communal Spaces," Architectural Record, n.d., https://digital.bnpmedia.com/publication/?i=751805&article_id=4299730&view=articleBrowser.

203 "PASSION CAN CREATE"
Le Corbusier, Towards a New Architecture (John Rodker, 1931), 4.

204 "I GREW UP WITH STEEL"
Interview by David Bruce Lee and Marina Bourderonnet, "Olson Kundig," n.d., FAME, https://www.famearchitects.com/blog/tom-kundig-architect.

204 "I ALWAYS TRY TO USE"
nterview by Donald Bates, "Alison Brooks Talks Architecture's 'Role in Making People Feel Valued,'" Architecture, Au, December 19, 2018, https://architectureau.com/articles/alison-brooks-talks-career-beginnings-award-winning-works-and-design-ideals/.

204 "I ALWAYS USE"
nterview by Ellie Stathaki, "Bernard Tschumi Q&A Exclusive," Wallpaper*, August 13, 2022, https://www.wallpaper.com/architecture/bernard-tschumi-qa-exclusive.

205 "WE CONSIDER COLOR"
Maria Cristina Didero, "Sauerbruch Hutton: Works for Munich," Domus, March 20, 2010, https://www.domusweb.it/en/nterviews/2012/03/20/sauerbruch-hutton-works-for-munich.html.

206 "I AM MORE INTERESTED"
Interview by Michael C. Y. Fei, Dialogue, no. 67 (March 2003), reprinted at https://ichaelfei.blogspot.com/p/forming-informal-conversation-with.html.

206 "MY WORKS"
Interview by Caroline Brand, "Santiago Calatrava's Extraordinary Designs," B Beyond, n.d., https://www.bbeyondmagazine.com/santiago-calatrava-interview-architecture-art-legacy/.

207 "I WORK WITH MUD"
Interview by Alison Cleary and Susie Ashworth; comp. and ed. Susie Ashworth, "In Conversation with . . . Yasmeen Lari," Parlour, August 31, 2018, https://parlour.org.au/series/in-conversation/in-conversation-with-yasmeen-lari/.

208 "IN A SENSE"
Interview by David Dick-Agnew, "Q&A: Sou Fujimoto on Building with Light," Azure, September 20, 2016, https://www.azuremagazine.com/article/interview-with-sou-fujimoto-forest-of-light-installation/.

208 "MY FAVORITE MATERIAL"
Interview by Sydney Franklin, Architizer in collaboration with Spirit of Space, n.d., https://architizer.com/blog/practice/materials/spirit-of-space-steven-holl-visual-arts-building.

209 "BAMBOO IS THE GREEN STEEL"
Amy Frearson, "Vo Trong Nghia Uses Bamboo Ladders to Build Pavilion at Sydney's SCAF Gallery," Dezeen, July 28, 2016, https://www.dezeen.com/2016/07/28/vo-trong-nghia-architects-green-ladder-pavilion-sherman-contemporary-art-foundation-scaf-sydney-fugitive-structures-series/.

209 "USING A MATERIAL"
Ted Loos, "From Divergence, a Thoughtful Calm," New York Times, March 28, 2014, https://www.nytimes.com/2014/03/30/arts/design/tadao-andos-new-work-at-the-clark-institute.html.

210 "IF DESIGNED AND INSTALLED"
Interview by Blaine Brownell, Architect, March 13, 2024, https://www.architectmagazine.com/practice/an-interview-with-pritzker-prize winner-riken-yamamoto_o.

210 "ALUMINUM"
Gio Ponti, In Praise of Architecture, trans. Giuseppina Salvadori and Mario Salvadori (F. W. Dodge, 1960), 130.

211 "GLASS TECHNOLOGY"
"Benedetta Tagliabue (Italy): Outside Space Is Also Home," Constructing a Sustainable Future, Saint-Gobain, n.d., https://www.constructing-sustainable-future.com/en/interviews/benedetta-tagliabue-outside-space-is-also-home/.

211 "GLASS IS ONE OF THE MOST"
"Subversion, Silence, and Normality," interview in Renzo Piano and Building Workshop: Buildings and Projects 1971–1989 (Rizzoli, 1989), 242.

211 "ANY WORK OF ARCHITECTURE"
Emilio Ambasz, The Architecture of Luis Barragán (The Museum of Modern Art, 1976), 8.

212 "IF YOU TALK TO A BRICK"
"On Brick," in Louis I. Kahn: Writings, Lectures, Interviews, ed. Alessandra Latour (Rizzoli, 1991), 295.

212 "BRICK HAS A SPECIAL RICHNESS"
Interview by Jesse Dorris, "Studio KO Journeys into Uzbekistan's History," Surface, June 6, 2023, https://www.surfacemag.com/articles/studio-ko-venice-biennale-uzbekistan-pavilion-interview/#.

213 "BRICKS WILL BE"
Vitruvius: The Ten Books on Architecture, trans. Morris Hicky Morgan, Book II (Harvard University Press, 1914), 43.

214 "I APPRECIATE"
"Odile Decq: ArchIdea 62 Interview," Forbo, December 2020, https://www.forbo.com/flooring/en-uk/inspiration-references/making-spaces-into-places-blog/odile-decq-archidea-interview/pgmrpu.

214 "SENSE EMERGES"
Peter Zumthor, "A Way of Looking at Things," in Thinking Architecture (Birkhäuser, 1999), 11.

215 "I AM OBSESSED"
Sophie Lovell, David Thulstrup: A Sense of Place (Phaidon, 2023), 112.

216 "GROWN, CAST, CUT"
Interview by Jon Astbury, Architects' Journal, February 7, 2018, https://www.architectsjournal.co.uk/news/stephanie-macdonald-of-6a-i-am-so-impressed-by-the-generations-of-women-coming-after-me.

216 "REGARDLESS OF WHAT"
Interview by Jack Murphy, "How Do You Hang an Auditorium from a Queen Post Truss?" Architect's Newspaper, October 21, 2022, https://www.archpaper.com/2022/10/grafton-architects-has-designed-its-first-building-in-north-america-to-be-a-masterclass-in-timber/.

217 "TIMBER IS A WONDERFUL MATERIAL"
Interview by Ingerid Helsing Almaas and Einar Bjarki Malmquis, "The Norwegian House," Arkitektur N, February 5, 2011, https://www.architecturenorway.no/stories/people-stories/andresen-10/.

217 "ONE OF THE FEW"
Andrea Oppenheimer Dean, "Interview with 2009 AIA Gold Medal Winner Glenn Murcutt," Architectural Record, May 16, 2007, https://www.architecturalrecord.com/articles/6029-interview-with-2009-aia-gold-medal-winner-glenn-murcutt.

217 "I PARTICULARLY LIKE"
Interview by Leeji Choi, designboom, May 1, 2009, https://www.designboom.com/interviews/shigeru-ban-designboom-interview/.

218 "FROM MY OWN HERITAGE"
Interview by Rebecca Herlemann and Antonina Krezdorn, Museum Folkwang, n.d., https://www.museum-folkwang.de/en/interview-yussef-agbo-ola.

218 "WHEN I SEE WOOD"
Interview by Stuti Agarwal, "Of Buildings and Belonging: Brinda Somaya on Buildings that Breathe and Travel that Teaches," Travel & Leisure India, August 29, 2025, https://www.travelandleisureasia.com/in/people/interview-with-architect-brinda-somaya/.

219 "WE ACTUALLY THINK"
Isla Sutherland, "Placemaking over Object-Making: Shim-Sutcliffe," Architecture, Au, January 16, 2023, https://architectureau.com/articles/shim-sutcliffe/.

220 "I WANT TO HAVE"
Interview by Y-Jean Mun-Delsalle, "Indian Architect Bijoy Jain Brings Studio Mumbai to Paris," Forbes, March 14, 2024, https://www.forbes.com/sites/yjeanmundelsalle/2024/03/14/indian-architect-bijoy-jain-brings-studio-mumbai-to-paris/.

220 "I REALLY LOVE"
"Tei Carpenter with Ayesha Ghosh," Brooklyn Rail, November 2024, https://brooklynrail.org/2024/11/architecture/tei-carpenter-with-ayesha-ghosh/.

221 "THE EXISTING BUILDING"
"Symposium Examines Strategies to 'Re-materialize' Construction," Holcim Foundation, April 4, 2019, https://www.holcimfoundation.org/media/news/forum/day-1-symposium-examines-strategies-to-re-materialize-constructi#:~:text="The%20existing%20building%20is%20tomorrow's,Forum%20held%20in%20Cairo%2C%202019.

MONEY

222 "THE IMPORTANCE"
Sam Lubell, "Shigeru Ban on His Masterfully Minimalist Interiors for Cast Iron House," Wallpaper*, October 13, 2022, https://www.wallpaper.com/architecture/shigeru-ban-interview-cast-iron-house-interiors-new-york-city-usa#:~:text=As%20for%20this%20foray%20into,to%20do%20with%20the%20budget.

223 "IF SOMEBODY COMES"
Interview by Alison Beard, "Life's Work: An Interview with Daniel Libeskind," Harvard Business Review, July–August 2018, https://hbr.org/2018/07/lifes-work-an-interview-with-daniel-libeskind.

223 "LUXURY IS LIGHT"
Ellie Stathaki, "Can Good Housing Be Accessible to All?" Wallpaper*, no. 268 (August 2021), reprinted at https://www.wallpaper.com/architecture/architect-fernanda-canales-on-housing-mexico ; originally published in August 2021 issue.

224 "WE NEVER COUNTED"
Julia Gamolina, "Constantly Looking: Farshid Moussavi on Creativity over Experience and Remaining Connected and Relevant," Madame Architect, August 8, 2019, https://www.madamearchitect.org/interviews/2019/8/6/farshid-moussavi.

224 "WE WORKED EVERY DAY"
Interview by Detlef Mertins, "Cracking the Glass Ceiling," SOM Journal, no. 4 (2006), reprinted at https://som.medium.com/cracking-the-glass-ceiling-a-look-back-at-the-career-of-trailblazing-architect-natalie-de-blois-b7ef02b28c2b.

225 "I FIND MYSELF"
John Cairney, The Quest for Charles Rennie Mackintosh (Luath Press, 2004), 193.

225 "I HATE TO ASK"
Frank Lloyd Wright to Dr. Ludd M. Spivey, February 11, 1939, in Letters to Clients, ed. Bruce Brooks Pfeiffer (Architectural Press, 1987), 173.

226 "I CAN'T HELP"
"Interview with Tsuyoshi Tane—vol. 2," Arts & Science, December 6, 2023, https://arts-science.com/en/editorial/tsuyoshitane_interview2/.

226 "I DON'T GIVE A FUCK"
Dana Goodyear, "The Iconoclast Remaking Los Angeles's Most Important Museum," New Yorker, October 5, 2020, https://www.newyorker.com/magazine/2020/10/12/the-iconoclast-remaking-los-angeles-most-important-museum.

227 "THE MEETING PLACE"
Interview by Felix Burrichter, PIN–UP, no. 24 (Spring/Summer 2018): 82–95.

227 "THE BIGGEST CHALLENGE"
Interview by Julia Gamolina, "Culture and Identity: Oshinowo Studio's Tosin Oshinowo on Calculated Risks, Apprenticeship, and Moving Forward," Madame Architect, January 31, 2024, https://www.madamearchitect.org/interviews/2024/1/16/tosin-oshinowo.

228 "WE'RE TRYING TO DO"
Interview by Antonio Pacheco, "Inside the Rising Mexico City–Based Practice of Frida Escobedo," Architect's Newspaper, February 28, 2017, https://www.archpaper.com/2017/02/frida-escobedo-emerging-voices/.

228 "THE LINE BETWEEN"
Quoted in Lincoln Caplan, "An Architecture of Possibilities," New Yorker, November 7, 1988, https://www.newyorker.com/magazine/1988/11/14/an-architecture-of-possibilities.

229 "I'M SCARED STIFF"
"Remarks," in Louis I. Kahn: Writings, Lectures, Interviews, ed. Alessandra Latour (Rizzoli, 1991), 191.

MUSEUMS

230 "A WHITE BOX"
Julian Rose, Building Culture (Princeton Architectural Press, 2024), 241.

231 "WHAT I LOVE"
Dale Berning Sawa, "A Profile of Annabelle Selldorf: 'I'm Not Afraid of Asserting Myself—but It's Not About Wanting to Be Powerful for the Sake of It,'" Art Newspaper, April 9, 2025, https://www.theartnewspaper.com/2025/04/09/a-profile-of-annabelle-selldorf-%7C-im-not-afraid-of-asserting-myselfbut-its-not-about-wanting-to-be-powerful-for-the-sake-of-it.

231 "WHEN I DESIGN"
"Kulapat Yantrasast—Architect," Genius List, n.d., https://www.thegeniuslist.com/interview/kulapat-yantrasast/.

231 "IN MUSEUMS"
Interview by Patricia Zohn, "Off the C(H)uff: Zaha Hadid and Her MAXXI Museum in Rome," Huffington Post, July 1, 2010, https://www.huffpost.com/entry/off-the-chuff-zaha-hadid_b_630345.

232 "DESIGNING FOR ART"
"Lina Ghotmeh Is Reimagining Cultural Architecture for a Connected World," Observer, December 29, 2025, https://observer.com/2025/12/interview-lina-ghotmeh-museums-architecture-global-dialogue/.

232 "A MUSEUM BUILDING CERTAINLY"
Walter Gropius, "Designing Museum Buildings," in Apollo in the Democracy: The Cultural Obligation of the Architect (McGraw-Hill, 1968), 141.

233 "A MUSEUM BUILDING SHOULD"
Julian Rose, Building Culture (Princeton Architectural Press, 2024), 267.

233 "I THINK THE BEST"
Interview by Fredi Fischli and Niels Olsen, "Stones, Inflatables, and Ephemera: The Chilean Architect's Fragile Vision of Architecture," PIN–UP, no. 37 (Fall/Winter 2024/25), https://www.pinupmagazine.org/articles/smiljan-radic-interview.

234 "SOMEBODY SAID"
The Mike Wallace Interview, September 28, 1957, https://hrc.contentdm.oclc.org/digital/collection/p15878coll90/id/81/.

234 "SOON AFTER"
Julian Rose, Building Culture (Princeton Architectural Press, 2024), 107

235 "A MUSEUM"
"Chris Dercon in Conversation with Jacques Herzog and Pierre de Meuron," in Tate Modern: Building a Museum for the 21st Century, ed. Chris Dercon and Nicholas Serota (Tate, 2016), 92–121.

NATURE

236 "HUMANS SEEM TO"
Interview by Shawn Adams, "Nlé's Kunlé Adeyemi: 'Humans Seem to Know More Abou Living on the Moon than the Ocean,'" Frame, March 31, 2023, https://frameweb.com/articl living/nles-kunle-adeyemi-humans-seem-to-know-more-about-living-on-the-moon-than-the-ocean.

237 "THERE IS NOTHING"
Interview by Ben Wheeler, "Wael Al Awar on the Future Vernacular," East East, n.d., https://easteast.world/posts/483.

237 "IN EACH HOUSE"
Interview by Lazar D. Kesic, "Rafiq Azam: The Poetry of Architecture and Watercolors of Bangladesh," AIA New York, August 14, 2014, https://www.aiany.org/news/rafiq-azam-the-poetry-of-architecture-and-watercolors-of-bangladesh/.

238 "WHEN I STARTED"
Interview by Tim Lewis, "Lord Norman Foster: 'I Still Get the Same Buzz from Designing Buildings,'" The Guardian, April 3, 2022, https://www.theguardian.com/artanddesign/2022/apr/03/lord-norman-foster-i-still-get-the-same-buzz-from-designing-buildings-.

238 "WITHOUT NATURE"
Interview by Sam Lubell, "Designed for Serenit with Nature in Mind," New York Times, October 10, 2019, https://www.nytimes.com/2019/10/10/arts/design/vo-trong-nghia-architecture.html.

239 "MORE AND MORE"
Interview by Isabelle Priest, "British Museum Western Range Architect Lina Ghotmeh on Her Life, Work, and Influences," Ribaj, Jun 6, 2023, https://www.ribaj.com/culture/interview-lina-ghotmeh-serpentine-pavilion 2023-beirut-paris-stone-gardens-hermes.

239 "IF I AM ANXIOUS"
Interview by Sini Rinne-Kanto, Institut Finlandais, June 1, 2018, https://www.institut-finlandais.fr/en/monthly-feature-june-2018-juhani-pallasmaa/.

240 "THE BIGGEST DEBATE"
Interview by Ana Vaz Milheiro, "Alejandro Aravena: 'Cities Play an Important Role in Correcting Inequalities,'" Electra, no. 21 (Summer 2023), https://electramagazine.fundacaoedp.pt/en/editions/issue-21/alejandro-aravena-cities-play-important-role-correcting-inequalities.

240 "EVERYTHING MAN IS"
Justin McGuirk, "Frei Otto: Icon 023," Icon, May 23, 2005, https://www.iconeye.com/back-issues/frei-otto-icon-023-may-2005.

241 "IT IS NOT ABOUT"
Interview by Robert Bevan, Australian, March 18, 2011, https://sydneyarchitecturearchive.wordpress.com/category/styles/modern-amorphic/.

241 "WHAT ABOUT HUMAN"
Interview by Victoria Camblin, PIN-UP, no. 36 (Spring/Summer 2024), https://www.pinupmagazine.org/articles/anupama-kundoo-interview.

242 "I LOVE"
Interview by Gustave Axelson, "What Is Missing? Q&A with Maya Lin," Cornell Lab: All About Birds, July 15, 2012, https://www.allaboutbirds.org/news/what-is-missing-qa-with-maya-lin/.

242 "BECAUSE I WAS FROM"
Interview by Guy Horton, "'The Future Is a Spreading Matrix': In Conversation with Sou Fujimoto," ArchDaily, November 21, 2018, https://www.archdaily.com/906059/the-future-is-a-spreading-matrix-in-conversation-with-sou-fujimoto.

243 "NO MATTER HOW BIG"
Interview by Isla Sutherland, "Placemaking over Object-Making: Shim-Sutcliffe," Architecture, Au, January 16, 2023, https://architectureau.com/articles/shim-sutcliffe/.

244 "I WATCHED"
Interview by Bailey Storey, "Hidden Canada: How Douglas Cardinal Brought Indigenous Perspectives into St. Mary's Catholic Church," Hidden Canada in collaboration with ACO NextGen and the University of Toronto, June 15, 2021, https://arthistory.utoronto.ca/news/hidden-canada-how-douglas-cardinal-brought-indigenous-perspectives-st-mary's-catholic-church.

245 "IT IS ALL ABOUT"
Interview by Jincy Iype, "Ma Yansong on Buildings of Freedom that Rethink Our Fellowship with Nature," Stir World, March 24, 2023, https://www.stirworld.com/inspire-people-ma-yansong-on-buildings-of-freedom-that-rethink-our-fellowship-with-nature.

245 "I UNDERSTAND"
Interview by Nile Greenberg, Brooklyn Rail, October 2024, https://brooklynrail.org/2024/10/architecture/peter-zumthor-with-nile-greenberg/.

PHILOSOPHY

246 "FORM EVER FOLLOWS"
"The Tall Office Building Artistically Considered," Lippincott's Magazine, March 1896, https://dn790003.ca.archive.org/0/items/tallofficebuildi00sull/tallofficebuildi00sull.pdf.

247 "THERE IS NO ARCHITECTURE"
Frank Lloyd Wright Foundation, https://frankllloydwright.org/frank-lloyd-wright/.

247 "EVERY REALLY GOOD ARCHITECT"
Interview by Corrado Curti, "ARCHITECTURE: The Solid State of Thought [Complete]," n.d., reprinted at https://lebbeuswoods.wordpress.com/2010/12/10/architecture-the-solid-state-of-thought-complete/.

248 "WE'RE NOT PRESERVATIONISTS"
Interview by Jason Farago, Even, no. 2 (Fall 2015), https://evenmagazine.com/elizabeth-diller/.

248 "I THINK THE WORD"
Interview by Markus Miessen, Bidoun, n.d., https://www.bidoun.org/articles/rem-koolhaas.

248 "I BELIEVE THAT IF PEOPLE"
Interview by Zdena Zednickova, "Between Nature and Architecture: Sou Fujimoto Discusses His Approach to Design," designboom, June 29, 2018, https://www.designboom.com/architecture/sou-fujimoto-interview-prague-resite-06-29-2018/.

248 "I BELIEVE SO MUCH"
Interview by Patricia McLaughlin, "How'm I Doing, Corbusier?" in Louis I. Kahn: Writings, Lectures, Interviews, ed. Alessandra Latour (Rizzoli, 1991), 300.

248 "WE GIVE THE SAME IMPORTANCE"
Interview by Myrto Katsikopoulou, "Inside MK27's Cinematic Architecture: Marcio Kogan Discusses New Rizzoli Monograph," designboom, May 29, 2024, https://www.designboom.com/architecture/marcio-kogan-mk27-cinematic-monograph-rizzoli-interview-05-29-2024/.

248 "MY WIFE'S PHILOSOPHY"
"The Green Blueprint," Prestige, July 13, 2024, https://theprestige.global/the-green-blueprint/.

248 "I TRY THROUGH MY WORK"
Interview by Josh Harris, "Re-building a Country: Mphethi M. Morojele on Indigeneity, Animist Architecture and Sending Off Nelson Mandela," Architecture, Au, August 15, 2018, https://architectureau.com/articles/re-building-a-country-mphethi-m-morojele-on-indigeneity-animist-architecture-and-sending-off-nelson-mandela/.

248 "LET'S NOT PRODUCE"
Gretchen Carr, "The Spiritual Resonance of Douglas Cardinal: How One American Indigenous Community Created a Symbol of Modern Resilience," Architecture, Culture, and Spirituality Forum, May 22, 2024, https://acsforum.org/the-spiritual-resonance-of-douglas-cardinal-how-one-american-indigenous-community-created-a-symbol-of-modern-resilience/.

249 "I FIRMLY BELIEVE"
Harriet Thorpe, "Word Building," World of Interiors, August 24, 2025, https://www.worldofinteriors.com/story/architect-richard-england-on-poetry.

250 "I WANT TO MAKE"
Toyo Ito, Forces of Nature, ed. Jessie Turnbull (Princeton Architectural Press; Princeton University School of Architecture, 2012), 128.

250 "A BUILDING THAT RELATES"
Interview by Romullo Baratto, "'It's Not Because You Are Limited in Resources That You Should Accept Mediocrity,'" ArchDaily, September 24, 2021, updated March 15, 2022, https://www.archdaily.com/968831/its-not-because-you-are-limited-in-resources-that-you-should-accept-mediocrity-interview-with-francis-kere.

250 "I BELIEVE"
Interview by Andrew Maerkle, "Architecture in Exhibition: Ryue Nishizawa," ART iT, September 1, 2010, https://www.art-it.asia/en/u/admin_ed_feature_e/vy0ppsjm8hmeniwflwnd/.

251 "BUILDINGS ARE KNOWLEDGE"
Interview by Stefan Novakovic, "Designing Agency: Lisa Landrum on Inclusive Architecture Education," Azure, June 10, 2024, https://www.azuremagazine.com/article/designing-agency-lisa-landrum-on-inclusive-architecture-education/.

251 "WE BELIEVE THE PROJECT"
Interview by Meghna Mehta, "Dreaming Reality," Mondo*arc India, no. 15 (July/August 2017), https://www.stirworld.com/inspire-people-dreaming-reality.

252 "HUMANISM IS PROBABLY"
Interview by Maria Spassov, "Michael Graves on Discovering Architecture, the Rewards of Practice, and the Most Important Element of Design," ArchDaily, June 2, 2015, https://www.archdaily.com/769558/michael-graves-on-discovering-architecture-the-rewards-of-practice-and-the-most-important-element-of-design.

252 "A GOOD DESIGN"
Rachel Elliot-Jones, "Keiji Ashizawa on Rebuilding a Less-Fragile Future," Assemble Papers, June 11, 2015, https://assemblepapers.com.au/2015/06/11/modesty-and-materiality-keiji-ashizawa/.

252 "IT'S IMPORTANT"
Y-Jean Mun-Delsalle, "Spotlight on Autoban, the Most Exciting Design Studio to Hail from Turkey in the Past Decade, Part 2," Forbes, March 25, 2017, https://www.forbes.com/sites/yjeanmundelsalle/2017/03/25/spotlight-on-autoban-the-most-exciting-design-studio-to-hail-from-turkey-in-the-past-decade-part-2/.

253 "I DON'T NEED"
Interview by Vladimir Belogolovsky, "Glenn Murcutt: 'Any Work of Architecture that Exists or Has a Potential to Exist Is There to Be Discovered,'" Curatorial Project, September 2013, http://curatorialproject.com/interviews/glennmurcutt.html.

QUESTIONS

254 "THERE ARE 360 DEGREES"
Simon Hattenstone, "Master Builder," The Guardian, February 3, 2003, https://www.theguardian.com/artanddesign/2003/feb/03/architecture.artsfeatures.

255 "TO ME, ARCHITECTURE"
Interview by Vladimir Belogolovsky, "Cecil Balmond Insists on Trying to Break the Formality of Any Order and Regularity," Stir World, September 13, 2021, https://www.stirworld.com/think-columns-cecil-balmond-insists-on-trying-to-break-the-formality-of-any-order-and-regularity.

255 "WE JUST KEEP COMING BACK"
Q&A moderated by Julie Eizenberg, "Andrew Freear and Rusty Smith, Rural Studio: The Challenges of Sustainable Rural Living," The Architectural League New York, September 13, 2022, https://archleague.org/article/andrew-freear-and-rusty-smith-transcript-rural-studio-the-challenges-of-sustainable-rural-living-transcript/.

256 "TO CREATE"
Quoted in Irene Sofia Comi, "Eileen Gray," Domus, March 24, 2023, https://www.domusweb.it/en/biographies/2023/03/24/eileen-gray.html.

257 "PRACTICING ARCHITECTURE"
Peter Zumthor, "Teaching Architecture, Learning Architecture," in Thinking Architecture (Birkhäuser, 1999), 57.

257 "HOW CAN I DESIGN"
Mimi Zeiger, "Take Care," Art Forum, September 2019, https://www.artforum.com/features/mimi-zeiger-on-the-architecture-of-diebedo-francis-kere-244409/.

257 "WITH THE INCREASING WORLD"
Interview by Cristiano Luchetti, Compasses, no. 37, n.d., https://compassesworld.com/interviews/material-an-interview-with-wael-al-awar/.

258 "IF YOU WALK DOWN"
Samanth Subramanian, "How Balkrishna Doshi Bent Le Corbusier's Modernism to the Needs of India," New Yorker, March 21, 2018, https://www.newyorker.com/culture/culture-desk/how-balkrishna-doshi-bent-le-corbusiers-modernism-to-the-needs-of-india.

258 "WHY SHOULD WE"
Interview by Alison Cleary and Susie Ashworth; comp. and ed. Susie Ashworth, "In Conversation with . . . Yasmeen Lari," Parlour, August 31, 2018, https://parlour.org.au/series/in-conversation/in-conversation-with-yasmeen-lari/.

259 "WHAT IF ARCHITECTS"
Interview by Vladimir Belogolovsky, "'Could Policy-Making Be be Considered Architecture?' A Q&A with Frida Escobedo," Azure, July 5, 2022, https://www.azuremagazine.com/article/frida-escobedo-interview-2022/.

SCALE

260 "I DON'T THINK"
Interview by Fredy Massad, ABC blog, https://abcblogs.abc.es/viga-en-el-ojo/otros-temas/interview-with-peter-eisenman.html.

261 "WHAT IS THE CHIEF"
"The Tall Office Building Artistically Considered," Lippincott's Magazine, March 1896, https://dn790003.ca.archive.org/0/items/tallofficebuildi00sull/tallofficebuildi00sull.pdf.

261 "WHAT IS DONE"
Interview by Alain Elkann, Alain Elkann Interviews podcast, January 12, 2020, https://www.alainelkanninterviews.com/jean-nouvel/.

262 "I DON'T THINK"
India Block, "'The Most Destructive Thing Is to Demolish a Building,' Says Nicholas Grimshaw," Dezeen, February 15, 2009, https://www.dezeen.com/2019/02/15/nicholas-grimshaw-interview-riba-royal-gold-medal-2019/.

262 "PEOPLE CAN BE SURPRISED"
Ellie Stathaki, "Can Good Housing Be Accessible to All?" Wallpaper*, no. 268 (August 2021), reprinted at https://www.wallpaper.com/architecture/architect-fernanda-canales-on-housing-mexico; originally published in August 2021 issue.

262 "SMALL ROOMS OR DWELLINGS"
Leonardo da Vinci's Note-Books, ed. Edward McCurdy (Empire State Book, 1923), 66.

263 "SMALL-SCALE MEANS"
Interview by Romullo Baratto, "'It's Not Because You Are Limited in Resources that You Should Accept Mediocrity,'" ArchDaily, September 24, 2021, updated March 15, 2022, https://www.archdaily.com/968831/its-not-because-you-are-limited-in-resources-that-you-should-accept-mediocrity-interview-with-francis-kere.

263 "WE WOULD LOVE"
Michael Kimmelman, "Alejandro Aravena, the Architect Rebuilding a Country," New York Times Style Magazine, May 23, 2016, https://www.nytimes.com/2016/05/23/t-magazine/pritzker-venice-biennale-chile-architect-alejandro-aravena.html.

264 "IT HAS BEEN SAID"
Frank Lloyd Wright: An Autobiography (Petaluma, CA: Pomegranate Communications, 2005), 141.

265 "IN OUR OFFICE"
Dan Howarth, "They Thought I Was a Troublemaker Says Zaha Hadid," Dezeen, December 18, 2014, https://www.dezeen.com/2014/12/18/zaha-hadid-architecture-education-women-miami/.

265 "I'M AS HAPPY"
"Building the Future: Jones Studio," Images Arizona, n.d., https://imagesarizona.com/building-the-future-jones-studio/.

266 "WHY SMALL AND LARGE"
"Harmony Between Man and Nature," in Louis I. Kahn: Writings, Lectures, Interviews, ed. Alessandra Latour (Rizzoli, 1991), 337.

266 "WE'RE NOT ONLY THINKING"
Interview by Joann Gonchar, Architectural Record, January 30, 2017, https://www.architecturalrecord.com/articles/12193-interview-with-jeanne-gang.

267 "IDEAS CAN MIGRATE"
Interview by Vladimir Belogolovsky, "'A Vase May Give a Shape to a Room,'" ArchDaily, September 29, 2020, https://www.archdaily.com/948643/a-vase-may-give-a-shape-to-a-room-in-conversation-with-john-wardle.

SUSTAINABILITY

268 "I LIKE TO THINK"
Interview by Marianna Guernieri, "'Mariam Kamara: We Are Not Using the Knowledge We Have that Is Centuries Old,'" Domus, June 10, 2019, https://www.domusweb.it/en/architecture/2019/06/10/mariam-kamara-we-are-not-using-the-knowledge-we-have-that-is-centuries-old.html.

269 "WE HAVE ABUNDANCE"
Interview by Victoria Camblin, PIN–UP, no. 36 (Spring/Summer 2024), https://www.pinupmagazine.org/articles/anupama-kundoo-interview.

269 "WE HAVE MOVED"
Interview by Jessie French, Union, n.d., https://unionmagazine.com/in-conversation-jessie-french-and-tosin-oshinowo/.

270 "TO REKINDLE"
Interview by Patrick Kasingsing, "The Future Is a Journey to the Past: A Conversation with Mario Cucinella," Kanto, December 20, 202 https://kanto.ph/voices/mario-cucinella/

271 "SUSTAINABILITY IS NOT"
Interview with Salma Samar Damluji, "An Integral Way of Thinking: Post-War Reconstruction in Yemen," Daw'an Architecture Foundation, n.d., https://www dawanarchitecturefoundation.org/Files/6th-Awards-Book-MEA-Interview-Salma-Samar-Damluji.pdf.

271 "TO HAVE CONTROL"
Interview by Emanuele Quinz, Domus, June 25, 2020, https://www.domusweb.it/en/speciali/domusfordesign/gallery/2020 antonio-citterio-im-not-interested-in-revolutionizing-or-surprising-but-rather-in getting-to-the-synthesis.html.

272 "FOR DECADES"
Interview by Martha Moskowitz, "Two Female Architects Are Reimagining Urban Renewal in Beirut," Frederic, October 25, 2024, https://fredericmagazine.com/2024/10/arine-aprahamian-anne-lacaton-rolex-mentorship/.

272 "NOT EVERY BUILDING"
Interview by Myrto Katsikopoulou, "Jeanne Gang at In Focus: Radical Repair at Triennal Milano," designboom, October 25, 2023, https://www.designboom.com/architecture interview-jeanne-gang-in-focus-radical-repair-world-around-cartier-triennale-milano-10-25-2023/.

273 "THERE IS NOTHING"
"Benedetta Tagliabue (Italy): Outside Space Is Also Home," Constructing a Sustainable Future, Saint-Gobain, n.d., https://www.constructing-sustainable-future.com/en/interviews/benedetta-tagliabue-outside-space-is-also-home/.

274 "THE TERM 'SUSTAINABILITY'"
Interview by Andrew Manns, CLADMag, no. 1 (2019), https://www.cladglobal.com/architecture-design-features?codeid=33511&source=home&p=4.

274 "THE DEFINITIONS OF GREENNESS"
Interview by Erin Tallman, ArchiExpo, August 5, 2024, https://emag.archiexpo.com qa-fernanda-canales-on-social-housing-and community-projects/.

275 "WE THINK"
Maria Cristina Didero, "Sauerbruch Hutton Works for Munich," Domus, March 20, 2010, https://www.domusweb.it/en/interviews/2012/03/20/sauerbruch-hutto works-for-munich.html.

275 "WE ARE MOVING"
"More," The Night of Ideas, organized by the French Institute of Chile, the La Moneda Cultural Center, and the Teatro a Mil Foundation, January 2023.

276 "WE SHOULD ALWAYS"
Interview by Rory Stott, "'In an Existing Structure You Have More Freedom': Jacob Van Rijs on #Reuse in Architecture," MVRDV, July 15, 2021, https://www.mvrdv.com/stack-magazine/3918/jacob-van-rijs-reuse-interview.

276 "IF WE DESIGN"
Interview by Jana Perković, "Glenn Murcutt on Touching the Earth Lightly," Assemble Papers, November 14, 2019, https://assemblepapers.com.au/2019/11/14/glenn murcutt-touching-the-earth-lightly/.

276 "EVENTUALLY EVERY SINGLE"
utobiographical Musings," in Conversations with Paolo Soleri, ed. Lissa McCullough (Princeton Architectural Press, 2012), 33.

277 "SUSTAINABILITY IN THE END"
nterview by Ana Vaz Milheiro, "Alejandro Aravena: 'Cities Play an Important Role in Correcting Inequalities,'" Electra, no. 21 (Summer 2023), https://electramagazine.fundacaoedp.pt/en/editions/issue-21/ejandro-aravena-cities-play-important-role-correcting-inequalities.

TEACHING

278 "OUR OFFICE ACTS"
nterview by Marcus Fairs, Icon, June 2004, tps://www.iconeye.com/back-issues/rem-koolhaas-icon-013-june-2004.

279 "I FEEL THAT BEING"
"1973: Brooklyn, New York," in Louis I. Kahn: Writings, Lectures, Interviews, d. Alessandra Latour (Rizzoli, 1991), 323; originally published in Perspecta (Yale Architecture), no. 19 (1982): 89–100.

279 "NO LITTLE KID"
"Advocating for Culture Change in Academia and Practice," Girl Uninterrupted, March 27, 2021, tps://www.girluninterruptedproject.com/conversations/2021/3/27/sarah-whiting.

280 "I LIKE TO THINK"
erview by Sam Lubell, Architect's Newspaper, March 5, 2012, https://www.archpaper.com/2012/03/neil-denari/.

280 "IT IS IMPORTANT"
Interview by Patricia Calzo Vega, "Japan chitect Keiji Ashizawa: Context, Community Key to Designing for Disaster," GMA News Online, August 3, 2016, https://www.gmanetwork.com/news/scitech/echnology/576218/japan-architect-keiji-ashizawa-context-community-key-to-designing-for-disaster/story/.

280 "IF YOU ARE GOING"
Interview by Andrew Maerkle, "Architecture of Involvement," ART iT, April 1, 2011, https://www.art-it.asia/en/u/admin_ed_feature_e/vwrvm6mt4gulfkqa0gkc/.

281 "TEACHING HELPS ME"
Interview by Merel Pit, "Nathalie de Vries: 'Role Models Help the Next Generation to Do What They Do Best,'" MVRDV, ugust 3, 2021, https://www.mvrdv.com/stack-magazine/2820/nathalie-de-vries-interview-mevr-de-architect; originally published at A.ZINE's Mevr. de Architect, December 8, 2020, https://a-zine.nl/2020/12/08/rolmodellen-helpen-de-volgende-generatie-te-doen-waar-ze-goed-in-zijn/.

281 "I THINK IT HAS BEEN CLEAR"
Interview by Antonio Pacheco, "Mónica once de León on the Future of Architectural censure," Archinect, June 29, 2020, https://chinect.com/features/article/150204718/m-nica-ponce-de-le-n-on-the-future-of-architectural-licensure.

282 "I START MY CLASS"
terview by Eliza Jordan, Whitewall, May 22, 2023, https://whitewall.art/design/tatiana-bilbao-believes-architecture-is-a-basic-human-right/.

282 "TEACHING IS ALSO LEARNING"
Interview by Aileen Kwun and Bryn Smith, Twenty Over Eighty: Conversations on a Lifetime in Architecture and Design (Princeton Architectural Press, 2016), 145.

282 "I SEE TEACHING"
"Q&A: RAIC Gold Medal Winner Brigitte Shim on Teaching, Experimentation, and Cross-Disciplinary Design," Daniels (University of Toronto John H. Daniels Faculty of Architecture, Design, and Landscape), June 23, 2021, https://www.daniels.utoronto.ca/news/thu-jun-24-2021-12am/qa-raic-gold-medal-winner-brigitte-shim-teaching-experimentation-and.

282 "I NEED TO TEACH"
Interview by Gabriella de Ferrari, Bomb, July 1, 2002, https://bombmagazine.org/articles/2002/07/01/ben-van-berkel/.

282 "I OFTEN TALK"
Interview by Sini Rinne-Kanto, Institut Finlandais, June 1, 2018, https://www.institut-finlandais.fr/en/monthly-feature-june-2018-juhani-pallasmaa/.

283 "I ALWAYS"
Interview by Emma Robertson, "Thom Mayne: 'They Want You to Be Left or Right,'" The Talks, n.d., https://the-talks.com/interview/thom-mayne/.

283 "THE BEST SATISFACTION"
Interview by Marie Davidová, Collaborative Collective, Archiweb, April 25, 2018, https://www.archiweb.cz/en/n/interview/interview-with-odile-decq.

284 "MY TEACHING"
"Karim Nader," Kontextur (kntxtr), November 2021, https://kontextur.info/project/karimnader.

284 "ON REFLECTION"
"Lesley Lokko on the Nomadic African Studio: Reimagining Education, Mobility, and the Future of Architecture," Africans Column, n.d., https://africanscolumn.com/lesley-lokko-on-the-nomadic-african-studio-reimagining-education-mobility-and-the-future-of-architecture/.

285 "I WANT"
Interview by Felix Burrichter, PIN–UP, no. 21 (Fall/Winter 2016/17), https://archive.pinupmagazine.org/articles/the-pinup-quote-amale-andraos.

285 "THIS YOUNGER GENERATION"
Interview by Veronica Simpson, "Architecture Is My Life and My Lifestyle, Everything Together," Studio International, June 13, 2025, https://www.studiointernational.com/index.php/marina-tabassum-architect-serpentine-pavilion-2025.

286 "I DRAW AND BUILD"
Brendan Gill, "Outside the Profession," New Yorker, September 26, 1953, https://www.newyorker.com/magazine/1953/09/26/outside-the-profession.

286 "I AM ABLE TO TEACH"
Interview by Vladimir Belogolovsky, Azure, June 8, 2023, https://www.azuremagazine.com/article/spiders-and-eagles-were-my-teachers-in-conversation-with-peter-stutchbury/.

287 "OUR JOB IS NO LONGER"
"Architecture and the Future," IROHA, November 16, 2022, https://theiroha.com/blogs/architecture/hitoshi-abe.

TIME

288 "TIME IS IMPORTANT"
"Kazuyo Sejima: She Can Foresee the Future," Gentlewoman, no. 1 (Spring/Summer 2010), https://thegentlewoman.co.uk/library/kazuyo-sejima.

289 "WHAT YOU"
Eero Saarinen on His Work, ed. Aline Saarinen (Yale University Press, 1962), 9.

289 "IT'S NOT ONLY ABOUT"
Interview by Lynette Lee, Even, no. 6 (Spring 2017), https://evenmagazine.com/ma-yansong/.

290 "THE MOST IMPORTANT THING"
"Souto de Moura and Pallasmaa in Dialogue," Arquitectura Viva, October 30, 2017, https://arquitecturaviva.com/articles/souto-de-moura-and-pallasmaa-in-dialogue.

290 "ALTHOUGH I WORK"
Interview by Alison Beard, "Life's Work: An Interview with Daniel Libeskind," Harvard Business Review , July–August 2018, https://hbr.org/2018/07/lifes-work-an-interview-with-daniel-libeskind.

291 "IT'S NOT JUST"
Interview by Veronica Simpson, "Architecture Is My Life and My Lifestyle, Everything Together," Studio International, June 13, 2025, https://www.studiointernational.com/index.php/marina-tabassum-architect-serpentine-pavilion-2025.

292 "EVERY BUILDING"
Interview by Yuki Sumner, "'Something Like Love': A Conversation with Níall Mclaughlin," Azure, December 7, 2022, https://www.azuremagazine.com/article/niall-mclaughlin-interview-magadalene-college-stirling-prize/.

292 "ARCHITECTURE IS EXPOSED"
Peter Zumthor, "A Way of Looking at Things," in Thinking Architecture (Birkhäuser, 1999), 24–25.

293 "TIME IS MANAGED"
Interview by Shumi Bose, "Anupama Kundoo and the Architecture of Happiness," Wallpaper*, August 17, 2022, https://www.wallpaper.com/architecture/anupama-kundoo-profile.

LAST PAGE

320 "THE LIFE OF ARCHITECTURE"
Interview by Emma Robertson, "Tadao Ando: 'There Is No Such Thing as Creation from Nothing,'" The Talks, n.d., https://the-talks.com/interview/tadao-ando/.

Acknowledgments
With thanks to the following for their contribution to the book: Deb Aaronson, Sara Bader, James Brown, Julia Hasting, Tanya Heinrich, Stephanie Holstein, Virginia McLeod, Rebecca Morrill, João Mota, Maisie Skidmore, Phoebe Stephenson, Ana Rita Teodoro, Emilia Terragni, Jonas Wanstock, Elaine Ward, and Jonathan Whale.

Phaidon Press Limited
2 Cooperage Yard
London E15 2QR

Phaidon Press Inc.
111 Broadway
New York, NY 10006

Phaidon SARL
55, rue Traversière
75012 Paris

phaidon.com

First published 2026

ISBN 978 1 83729 253 0

A CIP catalogue record for this book is available from the British Library and the Library of Congress.

Commissioning Editor: Deb Aaronson
Project Editor: Maisie Skidmore
Production Controller: Elaine Ward
Design: Julia Hasting
Typesetting: Cantina

Printed in China

THE LIFE OF
ARCHITECTURE DOES
NOT END WHEN
ITS CONSTRUCTION
IS COMPLETED.
IT CONTINUES TO GROW
AND BE NURTURED
AFTER IT IS BUILT.
ALL THE WORKS
OF ARCHITECTURE
I HAVE DESIGNED ARE
STILL IN THE PROCESS
OF GROWING.

TADAO ANDO